Tune In

Hearing God's Voice
Through the Static

A Modern Girl's Bible Study
Refreshingly Unique

JEN HATMAKER

NAVPRESS

Discipleship Inside Out™

NAVPRESS

Discipleship Inside Out™

NavPress is the publishing ministry of The Navigators, an international Christian organization and leader in personal spiritual development. NavPress is committed to helping people grow spiritually and enjoy lives of meaning and hope through personal and group resources that are biblically rooted, culturally relevant, and highly practical.

For a free catalog go to www.NavPress.com
or call 1.800.366.7788 in the United States or 1.800.839.4769 in Canada.

www.navpress.com

NAVPRESS and the NAVPRESS logo are registered trademarks of NavPress. Absence of ® in connection with marks of NavPress or other parties does not indicate an absence of registration of those marks.

ISBN 978-1-57683-893-8

Cover design by Wes Youssi, The DesignWorks Group
Cover photo by George Diebold
Creative Team: Terry Behimer, Karen Lee-Thorp, Collette Knittel, Kathy Mosier, Arvid Wallen, Kathy Guist

Some of the anecdotal illustrations in this book are true to life and are included with the permission of the persons involved. All other illustrations are composites of real situations, and any resemblance to people living or dead is coincidental.

Unless otherwise identified, all Scripture quotations in this publication are taken from the HOLY BIBLE: NEW INTERNATIONAL VERSION® (NIV®). Copyright © 1973, 1978, 1984 by International Bible Society. Used by permission of Zondervan Publishing House. All rights reserved. Other versions used include: the *New American Standard Bible* (NASB), © The Lockman Foundation 1960, 1962, 1963, 1968, 1971, 1972, 1973, 1975, 1977, 1995; *the King James Version* (KJV). All italics are the author's. The study is best followed using an NIV Bible.

Printed in the United States of America

7 8 9 10 / 15 14 13

To Jesus, whose sacrifice revolutionized the availability of God's voice. Thank You, Friend. I'll never forget who brought me to this place.

Contents

Acknowledgments

More than anyone, Brandon, you really felt the sting of my new status: *employed*. Thank you for being the single mom around here for weeks without complaining. And thanks for being patient when I bit your head off for nothing. I'm sorry. I was really tired that month. I love you.

Much love to my Thursday night girls; thank you for sharing Luke, love, Passover. It is a joy to be surrounded by women who hear God's voice. My well never runs dry with you. And thanks for not making me plan our snacks and parties. As a result, now we have snacks and parties.

I'm always grateful to my editor, Karen Lee-Thorp. Your tolerance for my adjectives and italics is stunning. Thank you for letting me be me, while still making me better. Editing my Modern Girl's stuff and a reference book on world religions at the same time is a feat only a really smart Yale grad could pull off.

And thank you to my parents, Larry and Jana King, who have listened to God their whole lives. I grew up expecting God to talk to me. This apple didn't fall far from the nuthouse, or something like that. I love you. (Move to Texas already. I'm sick of paying for babysitters.)

Introduction

Hi, Modern Girls. I'm so glad you're here, tuning in to God with this silly, sarcastic girl as your program host. In researching this topic, I read a lot of stuff written by seminary professors and theologians. I drank whole pots of coffee just to get through some of it. So what am I doing in the company of these scholars? I'm just a Modern Girlfriend with a sassy mouth. MGs aren't into Old School. We're into progress and Starbucks.

And that's just it. Sometimes when wading through the depths of God, like how humanity can possibly hear divinity, we'd rather have one arm around a Girlfriend. I'm surely no theologian. And lucky for us, I don't talk like one either. This is a study that balances truth with humor for the Modern Girls out there. Frankly, I hope to make you wet yourself at least once. At the same time, we'll walk together through over twenty ways God speaks to His children. Twenty ways! It's amazing to hear the same voice that spoke the world into existence call your name.

The Bible quotations in this study are mostly from the NIV, but you can use any version. You will need a journal or notebook, preferably with lines in it, to write your answers to the questions. Most of these are what-does-this-have-to-do-with-your-life questions, so unless you're a girl of very few words (which most MGs aren't), you'll need more than half an inch in the book to respond.

You'll encounter three icons throughout the study representing three different ways to respond. The radio icon indicates a time to dig into the Word, the rearview mirror icon offers a chance to personally reflect on truth, and the telephone icon opens the door to intimate prayer.

I hope these next six weeks will forever change the way you communicate with God. Guess what? He's a talker. I knew I was made in His image.

Let's tune in together.

WEEK ONE

Say What?

Does God Still Speak?

When I was nine, my parents took me on my first ski trip. Besides falling asleep on Brett Coyle's shoulder on the bus ride (a high point during my awkward stage), I only remember one other thing: ski school. What little self-esteem I'd amassed on Brett's shoulder was promptly extinguished by spending the day on my face, unaware of the frozen snot pooled under my nose. That awkward status was as secure as Fort Knox.

In ski school, I remember wanting to stick to my instructor like a contagious disease. He was my only security. He'd ski in front of me, modeling how to hold my skis and telling me when to turn. His voice constantly led me: "Now left, Jen. Left. Left! GO LEFT! WEDGE!" I was a marginal student.

Toward the end of the morning, he sent me down the slope on my own. I remember the horror like it was yesterday. I felt so alone. I wanted him to tell me what to do. I wanted to imitate him as he skied in front of me. But all I heard was silence. By the time I slid to the bottom, I was done. I yanked those skis off and marched into the lodge, where I dropped on the nearest couch and cried my eyes out.

When my dad found me, the drama had escalated. "Ski school sucks, Dad! I'm not going back! The teacher left me all alone, and I don't know how to ski by myself!" My dad, full of mercy, picked me up by the bibs and booted me back to ski school quicker than you can say "a waste of $100." I remember what he said, too:

"Your teacher is still on that slope waiting to teach you. You're the one who left."

You know what I've discovered? Many believers feel like this when it comes to hearing God. His voice feels silent. His instruction seems absent. His presence is a question mark. Life is a slippery slope, and we want to hear our Teacher loud and clear.

But we don't.

And to make matters worse, all we *do* hear these days is "God told me this" and "God told me that." What? What are they hearing that we're not? God's voice seems like a mystery, or at best, a special privilege reserved for the chosen few. There is nothing more polarizing in Christian circles than the dividing line between the hearing and the deaf. It is altogether frustrating.

What are God's intentions? What is real? Does He still speak, and if so, is that voice for everyone? And if it is, why do only some believers seem to hear it? Let's look at two factors today and discover the God of conversation.

*Read Isaiah 55:1-3. What can you learn about God's intentions for conversation from these verses?

What kinds of things do you think God has in mind when He speaks in verse 2 of "what is not bread" and "what does not satisfy"?

How do you think those things get in the way of our hearing God?

The Word is one massive testimony to God's voice. From the first to last page, it declares God's voice as clear, deliberate, and understandable.

To Adam: "The LORD God *called* to the man, 'Where are you?' He answered, '*I heard you* in the garden'" (Genesis 3:9-10).

To Noah: "So God *said* to Noah, 'I am going to put an end to all people, for the earth is filled with violence because of them.'" Was that clear? Well, "Noah did everything just as God commanded him" (Genesis 6:13,22).

To Abram: "The LORD *had said* to Abram, 'Leave your country, your people and your father's household and go to the land I will show you.'" Say what? "So Abram left, as the LORD had *told him*" (Genesis 12:1,4). Apparently, it was understandable.

To Saul: "He fell to the ground and heard *a voice say* to him, 'Saul, Saul, why do you persecute me?' 'Who are you, Lord?' Saul asked. 'I am Jesus, whom you are persecuting'" (Acts 9:4-5).

Does this sound like a God who wasn't talking? Or did He talk in riddles? No, He constantly begged His people to listen, hear His voice, open their ears hundreds of times in Scripture. In turn, the faithful—and the potentially faithful—heard His words clearly. Obedience was not a matter of discernment, but of choice. This communication was a consistent feature of faith—God, and the people who loved Him, talked and listened. In fact, if Jesus represents any form of truth to you, hang your hat on His words: "Man does not live on bread alone, but on every word that comes from the mouth of God" (Matthew 4:4).

*List as many reasons you can think of as to why God would want a conversational relationship with every believer.

So what about those Bible people who heard Him so clearly? Weren't they extremely exceptional? Didn't they have special capabilities or something? Let's take a snapshot of the types of folks God talked to. The references are provided, but you don't need to look them up. Just consider their basic descriptions:

Samuel:	a prepubescent boy	(1 Samuel 3:1-14)
Gideon:	the terrified baby of his mediocre family	(Judges 6:14-15)
Abigail:	housewife of a loser	(1 Samuel 25:32-33)
Hosea:	victim of adultery	(Hosea 1:2)
Amos:	a sheepherding fig picker	(Amos 7:14-15)
Peter, Andrew, James, and John:	fishermen	(Matthew 4:18-21)
Matthew:	a Jewish tax collector for the Romans	(Matthew 9:9)
Ten lepers:	ten lepers	(Luke 17:11-19)

What do the commonalities of these listeners tell you about God?

Now, did these folks make an impact for the kingdom? Sure they did. But as Dallas Willard points out in *Hearing God*, "Aside from their obviously unique historical role, however, they are not meant to be exceptional at all. Rather they are examples of the normal human life God intended for us: God's indwelling

His people through personal presence and fellowship."[1]

The regular people He spoke to support this conclusion. I'm not the highest heel in the closet, but when God said, "He who has an ear, let him hear what the Spirit says to the churches" (Revelation 2:7), it seems anyone who has ears is fair game. Go on. Reach up there. Do you have one? Two even? Guess what—you're in the mix.

*What is your real experience of hearing God's voice? Loud and clear? Fuzzy? Silent? How do you feel about this whole thing?

Let's look at one other indicator that God is chatty. Lucky for us, we have the Word that tells the story from the beginning of mankind to Jesus' generation. Love it. We see clearly how He dealt. But I can't find one single verse or allusion or reference anywhere that God planned on going silent at the close of the written Word. If He intended on becoming mute as soon as Revelation was penned, He sure didn't give us any warning.

In fact, He said the exact opposite. Some of the most profound teaching on God's voice is in Isaiah, where it was made abundantly clear.

Flip back to Isaiah 48:16. What does God seem to be saying about the timing of His voice?

"At the time it happens, I am there." This truth doesn't have a statute of limitations. There is no expiration date on His presence. And, as if to emphasize His point, He urged, "Come near me and *listen* to this." Is God crazy? Is He playing some mean joke on us? Does He tell us to listen to Him, then hide in silence and laugh at us? Look, I'm convinced God is very funny, but He doesn't play like that.

Girls, the entire testimony of believers from Jesus' generation to this day cries out in favor of God's voice. If He went mute, then we're all a bunch of lunatics. I, for one, am definitely insane as I constantly "do what the Voices tell me." Comedian Lily Tomlin once said, "Why is it that when we speak to God we are said to be praying, but when God speaks to us we are said to be schizophrenic?"

As God's church, we have the richest history of divine conversation. The stories of God's leadership and the victories it has wrought are endless. God's conversations with His people mark the essence of our faith.

Billy Graham wrote an account of his calling while he was in college:

> But did I want to preach for a lifetime? I asked myself that question for the umpteenth time on one of my nighttime walks around the golf course. The inner, irresistible urge would not subside. Finally, one night, I got down on my knees at the edge of one of the greens. Then I prostrated myself on the dewy turf. "Oh God," I sobbed, "if you want me to serve you, I will." The moonlight, the moss, the green, the golf course—all the surroundings stayed the same. No sign in the heavens. No voice from above. But in my spirit I knew I had been called into the ministry. And I knew my answer was yes. From that night in 1938 on, my purpose and objectives in life were set. I knew I would be a preacher of the Gospel.[2]

 Have you ever heard God clearly? If so, describe your experience.

If not, any ideas why?

Girls, God's arrangement with us is not as mere benefactor,

nor is it simply stern judge. He doesn't hold us at arm's length. Nothing in His Word or history supports that conclusion. He calls us: friends, dear children, beloved, bride. And when do two friends not speak? What parent fails to instruct his child? Who withholds intimate communication from the object of his affection? What bride receives silence from the one who courted her? It's inconceivable that a God who lavished us with such terms of endearment would not speak to us.

So why does He seem silent for so many? Remember what my dad told me as I suffered as the fourth-grade martyr? "Your teacher is still waiting on that slope to teach you. You're the one who left." Oh Girls, if you don't know the gentle sound of God's voice, welcome to a journey that will leave you breathless. Your Teacher has always spoken, still speaks in this moment. You just have to learn to hear Him. Let's link arms together and discover that "God's voice thunders in marvelous ways; he does great things beyond our understanding" (Job 37:5).

Thunder on, God.

We're listening.

"Give ear and come to me;
   hear me, that your soul may live." (Isaiah 55:3)

Do you know the beauty of God's voice? Is it little more than a mystery? Thank God today for placing you on this journey, however you got here. Ask Him to begin the work of opening your ears, and commit to pursuing divine conversation.

The Battle of Wills

My Girlfriend Jenny is a bit obnoxious, God love her, which is clearly why we get along. For example, she called me three times a day for two weeks as she hunted for the perfect pair of cowgirl boots. I'm not kidding. She confessed that when the search was over, she asked her Bible study group to pray for her because she was so tired from shopping. I couldn't make this stuff up.

Jenny has fantastic taste, but for some reason she requires The Ten Concentric Levels of Confirmation on every purchase, then grieves in buyer's remorse regardless. Her special trick when she's torn between two items is to buy them both, hold someone hostage in the Ten Levels, and take one back the next day. The customer service counters hate her. She sucks me into her faux dialogue at least once a week:

> Jenny: Come look at the two shirts I bought to match
> that skirt I didn't take back last week.
> Jen: Which skirt?
> Jenny: Remember? The one that was 1/8 inch longer
> than the other one exactly like it that I returned?

Jen: Didn't I tell you to keep the other one?

Jenny *(ignoring Jen's question)*: Which of these shirts is cuter to match it?

Jen *(looking hard at each shirt; trying to tell which one Jenny already liked better; trying to develop telepathy)*: This one.

Jenny: What? I can't believe you picked that one! The other one is so much cuter! It's so obvious! I thought for sure you would know that! This one is so school marm! Isn't it? I mean, this is so not the one I thought you'd choose!

Jen *(deadpanning)*: The other one.

Jenny: Are you sure?

Jen: You're killing me.

Jenny is just that kind of girl who wants to hear what she wants to hear (and by "that kind of girl," I mean she is a girl). I can relate. While Girlfriends were made for this brand of dialogue, it doesn't roll with God. If we are only after His voice as long as He is saying what we want to hear, guess what He's going to say?

Nothing.

This takes on several shapes. Sometimes we're after a specific answer, but more often than not, we're after *some answer*. That's usually what we seek God for. Tell us what to do. Tell us which to choose. We want to boil down God's voice to a gimmicky formula that will work like a Ouija Board. Will it go to yeeesssss? Will it go to nooooo? This is what we need Him for: to sprinkle enlightenment upon our decisions to make us happier, successful, and "in God's will."

Ah, yes. In God's will. We love this phrase. I've heard it used with such blatant disregard for its full meaning that

Jesus would be rolling over in His grave (were He still there). Present company included, Girls. For me, this was usually in well-intentioned ignorance. Decision-making time seemed to be the best opportunity to get myself smack dab in the center of God's will. Wherever that was.

 When you hear "in God's will," what do you think of? Circumstances? Decisions? Location? Lifestyle?

Let's think of God's will in parenting terms. In my family, I talk pretty much from the moment my youngest wakes me up in the morning to the time I yell, "The next kid who gets out of bed is getting put on eBay tomorrow! *No reserve!*" (My patience has often run dry by eight o'clock in the evening.) Some are big directives: "No, a fire cannot be controlled if it is set in the bathtub. Give me those matches." Some are simple observations: "Underwear really serves its purpose better under your shorts." But in one way or another, they all matter.

If my kids listened only to certain directives while ignoring the others in the course of one day, at least two of them would die before sundown—either by their own hand or mine. I guarantee it. Yes, I am sometimes there to tell them what to do. But I also teach them kindness and a strong work ethic. I offer protection even when they think they are safe. Every disappointment they face is a teaching moment for me. Sometimes I communicate with no other objective than to lavish them with my love. Although they would surely disagree, telling them *what to do* is only a tiny fraction of my daily communication.

*If this is how God parents us, what are we missing when we seek His voice only to help us make a certain choice?

Read 1 John 2:15-17. What kinds of things stand in opposition to God's will? Try to put them into your own words.

Name some areas where you've wished or asked to know God's will.

John made it clear for us: "The world and its desires pass away, but the man who does the will of God lives forever." Oh Girls, God wants to teach us patience, but all we want to hear is whether to move to Atlanta or Houston. He wants to train us in integrity and righteousness, but we're only listening for a "yes" or "no." Or we're so single-mindedly focused on a desire that will pass away that we have entirely missed what it means to be in the will of a holy God.

Henry Blackaby put it like this:

When we listen for God's voice, what are we seeking? Is it answered prayer in which God merely grants our request? Is it his praise for the Christian services we perform? Is it guidance to help us carry out the plans we're making?

Certainly God does bless us beyond our due. He also affirms his children and gives us wisdom when we need it. But God's purposes are not the same as ours. We want him to indulge us; he wants to transform us.[3]

 In what ways, if any, do you identify with what Blackaby says?

God's will—what it really is—is demonstrated plainly in His Word, but we have to accept all of Scripture, not just the parts we like. For example, see what you can learn about God's will from the following passages:

Do not conform any longer to the pattern of this world, but *be transformed* by the renewing of your mind. Then you will be able to test and approve what *God's will* is—his good, pleasing and perfect will. (Romans 12:2)

We want you to know about the grace that God has given the Macedonian churches. Out of the most severe trial, their overflowing joy and their extreme poverty welled up in rich generosity. For I testify that *they gave as much as they were able*, and even beyond their ability . . . they urgently pleaded with us for the privilege of sharing in this service to the saints. And they did not do as we expected, but they gave themselves first to the Lord and then to us *in keeping with God's will*. (2 Corinthians 8:1-5)

Give thanks in all circumstances, for *this is God's will* for you in Christ Jesus. (1 Thessalonians 5:18)

Submit yourselves for the Lord's sake to every authority instituted among men. . . . For *it is God's will* that by doing good you should silence the ignorant talk of foolish men. (1 Peter 2:13,15)

So then, those who *suffer according to God's will* should commit themselves to their faithful Creator and continue to do good. (1 Peter 4:19)

*From the earlier passages, what does God want to produce in the lives of believers who follow His whole will?

Girls, *this* is the will we have to pursue in hearing God's wonderful voice. His whole will. It goes well beyond the boundaries of a "yes" or "no." The audible can only be turned up within the context of a life of obedience—even when it includes massive sacrifice. If you're here to find a formula to secure timely answers from God, please toss this book in the garbage, drive to Barnes & Noble, and find a good book on the Prosperity Gospel. There are plenty to choose from. Use your club card and save 10 percent.

This journey is founded on a paradigm shift: Not how does God's will fit into my life, but how does my life fit into God's will? This is the believer who can hear God's voice. The one He knows will listen. The one who wants to hear His voice no matter what it is saying. The one who plans on living His will, not just borrowing pieces of it. Together, we'll dive into hearing God not only for guidance, but to *know* Him. Oh Girls, let's become like Paul when he declared, "I consider everything a loss compared to the surpassing greatness of knowing Christ Jesus my Lord" (Philippians 3:8).

So far, is your pursuit of God's voice to speak to your agenda or to direct your whole life? Somewhere in the middle? Truthfully describe your current reality.

As His children, God has big plans for us. He won't be our magic Genie granting us answers for circumstances while remaining silent elsewhere, because He is after the whole of us. He wants our conversations to be marked by discussion, truth, laughter, discipline, compassion, revelation, and mutual adoration. And as a result, we are given the privilege of the whole of Him. The sacrifice, submission, even suffering of truly living in God's will is returned a hundredfold when each day is begun with His clear voice:

"Good morning. I have so much planned for you today."

Do you need to reorient your life in God's will? Ask Him to begin the paradigm shift in your heart from using Him to better your life to using your life to fulfill His will. Ask if there is a specific agenda item you need to release.

Deafening Silence

As any mom knows, it takes an act of God to get anything done around the house when your kids are there. The distractions are endless. The maintenance is constant. Not one day have I looked around and said, "Man, I don't have anything to do. I should get a job." At this moment, while I'm at my desk writing, I have one pile of laundry unfolded next to me, one in the dryer, one in the washer, an unmade bed behind me, a daughter I bribed downstairs with crafts, and a three-year-old I'm hoping is still in the house.

That's reality. So anytime it dawns on me that I've been working *without* interruption, I am afraid. Very afraid. A slow panic spreads, and I weigh the options of (1) continued silent productivity, or (2) finding that my boys have pried open a paint can and repainted the fireplace lime green. If I experience any period of silence in my house, there is a reason.

There is always a reason.

And I will pay dearly for it.

Girls, if God's voice seems silent, there is a reason. For believers, God's silence indicates that something is wrong. And I'm not pointing any fingers, but out of the two of you, only one is perfect. So if there is a guilty party—well, let's just say it's not God. Okay, it's you. And it's me. Communication between humanity and divinity comes with a built-in set of hearing blocks. Let's look at the two main obstructions today and begin the journey of tuning in to God's voice.

Sin

I'd love to skip this, but it stands as the number one hindrance to hearing God, so we'd better go there. Believer, we often want God's blessings but are unwilling to sell out to Him. Sin ruins everything. It destroys physically, spiritually, emotionally. It falsely elevates self over God. It perpetuates selective discipleship, which is not discipleship at all. Is there any way God would speak to us when we're choosing sin over Him?

My heart has broken as I've listened to believers rage against a God who has gone silent in their pain, when sin is the obvious culprit—either theirs or someone else's. Relationships lie in ruins, poor decisions haunt our dreams, sin goes unconfessed while we yell, "Where are You, God? You've left me!" Please hear this: We must accept that our sin will halt communication with God until we allow Him to deal with it. Period.

Read Isaiah 1:15-17. What was God teaching Israel about their prayers?

*This is hard truth, but it's still true. Why do you think it has to be this way?

When we think of sin, we often think of personal, private things. Why do you suppose justice for the oppressed and care for the weak (verse 17) was such a big deal to God?

If you've dealt with someone who is completely irrational

and refuses to own up to his or her faults, then you know what God is up against with a believer in sin. Any healthy conversation must be at least grounded in truth, or in God's economy, or it's not going to happen. He requires our honesty. How can He speak to us when we're pretending? What is even the point of having that conversation? We can't ask God for the goods while ignoring the elephant in the room.

Fortunately, sin—though ugly—will always be forgiven. Always.

Read Isaiah 1:18-19. From this section and the previous one, what can you detect in God's tone? What is His heart saying?

Do you have sin that is holding back God's voice? Or are you blaming some circumstance on God's silence when someone else's sin is at fault? If you are willing, stop and confess it right now. God's been waiting.

Spiritual Immaturity

Aren't newborns fun? Of course, I thought I would collapse under the pressure of our first, but I now know (after two more) those were the easiest years of my life. I loved how my oldest turned at the sound of my voice. Gavin could be across the room as an infant, but when he heard me talk, he'd crane his neck until he found me. It was one of those memories that replaced breast engorgement and convinced me to have another baby.

In fact, I could recite the Declaration of Independence, but as long as it was in my Mommy Voice, he loved it. He had no idea what I was saying. He knew the *sound* of my voice but was too little to understand the words. It wasn't long, though, and he understood everything I told him, even before he could speak. Now, at seven, he just ignores me, but that's a function of choice, not ability.

As young believers, we're like newborn babies. We can discern the sound of God's voice as He has called us, forgiven us. We recognize the kind quality of it and the tone that won us over, but learning to understand His words simply takes time. Experience develops an ear for Christ, and it cannot be short-circuited. In Scripture, the clarity of the message almost always indicated the spiritual condition of the hearer.

Make no mistake: New believers can develop this quickly if they are willing. Dallas Willard says, "Only our *communion* with God provides the appropriate context for *communications* between us and him."[4] Communion is a function of commitment. We'll reap what we sow here. A believer in fellowship with God will soon move beyond voice recognition to understanding.

On the other hand, there are believers who met God ages ago but haven't progressed in spiritual maturity at all. Their knowledge of God's Word and participation in His work is hardly different than the day they met Him. Often, His silence simply shows how little we are engaged in His business. How can you be trusted with God's secrets if you barely know Him?

*The Bible suggests a quick learning curve. Read Hebrews 5:11-14. From this text, what comparisons can you make between an older child and a maturing believer?

The following questions might shed some light on your spiritual maturity and, consequently, God's voice to you:

- To what use would I put a word from God?

- What has His clear word to me accomplished for His kingdom thus far?
- Would He find me faithful? Are we even in business together?
- What would I do if He asked me to change? Sacrifice? Obey?
- What *good* would it do for God to speak to me?

You only go to a dry well a few times before you find one that will produce. The words of God are sacred, holy, immeasurable. They are reserved for believers who are digging into Scripture, searching out holiness. He seeks the pure hearted who won't mismanage His directives. Hear this: He doesn't need us to be perfect, just willing. "The eyes of the LORD move to and fro throughout the earth that He may strongly support those whose heart is completely His" (2 Chronicles 16:9, NASB). Your spiritual progress is the conduit by which God talks clearly.

How do you answer some of the questions listed above? What good would it do God to speak to you?

Would you say you're moving forward spiritually, falling backward, or stuck? If you need to, and you're willing, stop and confess this to God. He walks forward with every willing believer.

Two quick words on some possible misunderstandings of "God's silence":

First, don't mistake softness for silence. I am particularly dense, so I'd love to hear God through, say, a megaphone. I keep telling Him that if He'd scream in my ear, I'd be very cooperative. I'm with Isaiah when he cried out, "Oh, that you would rend the heavens and come down" (Isaiah 64:1). I don't really know what *rend* means, but I'm all for this kind of display. There will come a day when every knee will bow at the sound of His voice, but for now, this is simply not His usual way.

He characterized His presence to Elijah not as a powerful wind tearing the mountains apart and shattering the rocks. Not as an earthquake breaking the very ground in half. Not as a fire charring everything in its path. No, God's presence came to Elijah as the sound of "a gentle whisper" (1 Kings 19:11-12). And as Solomon taught us, the spirit of mankind is searched by "the candle of the LORD" (Proverbs 20:27, KJV) — not a raging inferno that overcomes by force, but a soft light.

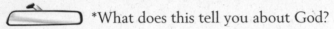 *What does this tell you about God?

If God had whispered to you during the past week, would you have noticed? Why or why not?

Second, just because God didn't answer the way you wanted doesn't mean He didn't answer. My three-year-old was recently stalling at bedtime and called me to his room (again). After he said he was scared to sleep for fear of nightmares, I suggested we pray. He clasped his little hands together and squeezed his eyes shut while I prayed: "God, please help Caleb have a great night's sleep. Will you take away all bad thoughts and give him happy thoughts? Amen." Caleb kept his eyes shut for a second, popped them open and said with a sigh:

"God said no."

Apparently a good night's sleep wasn't in God's will for Caleb. Life is sometimes hard like that.

Why do we only share "answered prayers" when we got what we asked for? What about when He said no? What about when He said wait? What about when He showed us a different way? What about when it became a teaching moment?

Why aren't those answers? When my children want something desperately, I'll only say no with good reason, and I'll help them understand why if they'll listen. So it is with God.

This was certainly true in the case of Paul's famous "thorn in the flesh," which he begged the Lord to remove from him three times. God was not silent, even though he turned down Paul's request: *"He said to me*: 'My grace is sufficient for you, for my power is made perfect in weakness'" (2 Corinthians 12:7-9). That was an answered prayer, Girls. Paul wanted relief. God wanted grace. Who knew best?

*Have you mistaken God's "no" or "wait" for silence in a specific situation? If so, describe your circumstance.

Did He whisper to you why He answered as He did? If so, were you willing to hear that? Why?

Now that we've looked at a few reasons why God might be silent (or appear to be), let me say this: He may choose silence for a reason that we cannot comprehend or have the privilege to know about. That's His prerogative. The day we can wrap our little arms around our infinite God, it's time to get a new God. He's bigger than us, thank goodness. He understands more than we do. Sometimes, His words are reserved until we're able to comprehend them. In His mercy — not His remoteness — He often gives us the time we need to grow into truth.

None of us really had any idea what we were getting into when we became parents. We couldn't look down the road far enough and anticipate the struggles. If we could, the human race might be extinct by now. With His words, God gives us what we can handle. If He allowed too much too soon, our fragility might render His words useless. The knowledge may stunt our growth. It's hard to manage "predestination" when we're still figuring out "grace."

We should remember that as we encourage new Christians. "New believer, meet God. He loves you." Let's start there. Systematic theology can wait awhile. With His disciples, Jesus was silent concerning His death until His final year. Smart, that One. Sometimes His silence is simply the gift of time.

So, with pure hearts, we can only open our hands toward heaven, admitting our errors and turning from them. We devour Scripture like it is the air we breathe. We adopt God's purposes, accepting the answers He sees fit to deliver. As much as it depends on us, we embrace sincere motives. We respond to each whisper, allowing them to increase in frequency and clarity. And if we encounter silence, we return to the last thing He told us, check our obedience, and wait for more.

> O God, do not keep silent;
> be not quiet, O God, be not still. (Psalm 83:1)

Are you hindering God's voice? Through sin? Apathy? Ask God to show you anything in your life that is muffling His voice. Pray for the strength to throw those things off. Ask Him to increase your sensitivity to His whispers and accept them when they come.

God?

My sisters, Lindsay and Cortney, and I make a good case for the milkman-father theory. You've never seen three sisters (biological, *or so we're told*) who look so different: our builds, our natural hair colors (though no one has seen those in ten years), the colors of our eyes. You wouldn't pick us out as related if ten million dollars were on the line.

Unless you get lucky and we open our big mouths to talk. We share the exact same voice. We talk the same; we sound the same. When any of us calls our mom, she never knows for a minute or two which daughter it is. She stays neutral at first: "Hi honey! How's it going? How's your week?" She has no clue.

She has to wait for some strong indicator: Jen = kids, Lindsay = work, Cortney = college. Unfortunately, any of us could say the same thing: "This week is ridiculous! I think I'm going crazy! I have PMS, and you know how I get." No help there. Sometimes she gets it wrong and starts asking me about my classes. I roll my eyes and say, "Mom, I've been out of college for ten years. Don't make me relive it. This is Jen."

If I've heard any one struggle regarding hearing God's voice, it's this: How do I know it's God? How do I know it's not me?

Or worse yet, the Enemy? Sometimes it all sounds the same, and discerning God's voice from its rivals can be daunting at best and disastrous at worst. Caller ID would be valuable in faith, and I've suggested it to God. He hasn't gotten back to me yet. So in the meantime, let's work through some strong indicators of God's voice, and learn to recognize them and notice when they're absent.

In human terms, what qualities distinguish one voice from another? What makes a voice familiar?

Quality

Let's look first at the *quality* of God's voice, His general manner of speaking. With humans, this marks the force of a voice: high, low, loud, soft, strong, subtle. It affects the way a voice is received. Well, I haven't heard God's actual voice, thank goodness. So how can we discern the quality of His voice? As the voices of Jesus and God are one and the same, we have physical examples of what to listen for from Scripture.

Read Matthew 21:23-27. Envision it. Put yourself there. What do you hear in Jesus' voice? How would you describe it?

This was not exceptional to the way Jesus spoke. It was the norm. He constantly had this effect on people, both His followers and enemies. Since we can't hear the timbre or depth of His voice, we can learn from how it was spoken and accepted.

We can distinguish the quality of His voice by the weight of authority with which it hits our souls as it comes to us through our thoughts. We are immediately impressed with the certainty of what He has said. Even against our nature, we are compelled to follow, bend, release, obey. When God speaks, it rings strong, and we sense inwardly its power. While the ramifications of His words may be confusing, the words themselves are not.

I love this: E. Stanley Jones said, "Perhaps the rough distinction is this: The voice of the subconscious argues with you, tries to convince you; but the inner voice of God does not argue, does not try to convince you. It just speaks, and it is self-authenticating. It has the feel of the voice of God within it."[5]

*Can you validate this with one of your experiences? When, if ever, has the *authority* of God's voice compelled you to a response?

Girls, God's word to you may be gentle, but it won't be weak. He speaks in strength. Hysterics are unnecessary. Let there be no mistake: What He says is right, and it will demand a response. You will understand why the demons responded immediately to Jesus' authority. It can't be helped.

Spirit

Beyond the strong quality of God's voice, it also bears a certain *spirit*. It's the spirit of a heavenly Parent who adores His children: loving, patient, jealous for our safety, protective, reasonable, so compassionate it almost hurts. So help me, this is God. We've distorted His voice and often expect disappointment—if He speaks to us at all. Please, please hear this: "There is now no condemnation for those who are in Christ Jesus" (Romans 8:1).

Stick a bookmark in Matthew 21, and read John 8:1-11. Can you hear it? What is the spirit of Jesus' voice? What is behind His words each time he speaks?

Oh, I know this spirit. This is the voice of Jesus. Believer, if you are hearing condemnation, that is certainly *not* the voice of God. He is incapable of speaking to you like that. Would you stand yelling over your daughter, declaring her a failure, as she cowered in the corner in shame? Would you recount her mistakes until they break her? Nor does God. You'll not hear that tone from Him.

The spirit of His voice strains toward our spiritual health. It gently mends what's broken. In mercy, it directs us back from our dangerous wanderings. It builds up, heals. As Jesus modeled, it's not permissive, as He loves us too much to leave us in our sin. Yet there is no condemnation. It remains intact in the midst of discipline. This spirit characterizes the voice of God.

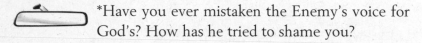 *Have you ever mistaken the Enemy's voice for God's? How has he tried to shame you?

In this spirit of health and wholeness, what have you heard from God? What has He tried to show you recently?

Content

Finally, God's voice is distinguished by the content of His words. While we might not initially recognize His voice based solely on what He says, this much we can know: God's directions will never contradict the truths of the Bible. He won't lead us in a way that harms His kingdom or destroys others. God doesn't speak contrary to His nature.

Look back over John 8:1-11 and Matthew 21:23-27. What principles of the Bible (such as love) does Jesus represent in His few words?

Know this: God won't ask you to hate, lie, cheat, judge. He won't have you cause dissention among His people. God wouldn't tell you to act in retaliation. He doesn't tempt you. He won't tell you to leave your husband unless you have biblical grounds to do so—and even then He'd rather heal your marriage. And God surely won't justify those if they happened to you. Don't believe "God told me to" on any of those assaults to His character.

Dallas Willard makes a fine distinction here: "In order to qualify as the voice of God, a thought, perception or other experience must conform to the principles—the fundamental truths—of Scripture. It is the *principles*, not the incidentals, of Scripture that count here. Study of the Scriptures makes clear that certain things are fundamental, absolute, without exception."[6]

Incidentals? For example, God told Moses as He led the whiny Hebrews: "Strike the rock, and water will come out of it for the people to drink" (Exodus 17:6). Well, you and I can strike as many rocks as we'd like, but I bet we won't see one drop of water. In Mark 10:21, Jesus told the rich young man to sell all his possessions for the poor in order to follow Him. This was an incidental, as Jesus didn't ask this specific act of obedience from everyone He talked to. He was speaking to the spiritual condition of this young man who elevated wealth above discipleship. Unless you have a crystal clear leading from the Spirit to obey an incidental in Scripture, you shouldn't take it as an absolute directive.

Yet when Jesus says, "Come to me, all you who are weary and burdened, and I will give you rest" (Matthew 11:28), we're onto a principle that is true for everyone. When Paul declares, "I consider everything a loss compared to the surpassing greatness of knowing Christ Jesus my Lord" (Philippians 3:8), that is a godly perspective that pops up from Genesis to Revelation. *Incidental*: "If a woman does not cover her head, she should have her hair cut off" (1 Corinthians 11:6). *Principle*: "Love your neighbor as yourself" (Mark 12:31).

An incidental passage of Scripture will *represent* a larger principle. This was true for Jesus' instruction to the rich young man. While God doesn't ask every believer to sell the farm, we're all to value God above the temporary. While He doesn't require every woman to cover her head, we're still to embrace modesty. No specific word from God will ever contradict the principles that permeate His Holy Word.

*Can you remember a time when God spoke to you and a biblical principle was clear? Forgiveness? Sacrifice? What was it?

Believer, if you know God's voice, then you are probably reading this—as my old school pastor used to say—"with a good hearty amen!" If you don't, I want to wrap my arms around your sweet neck and tell you that once the words of God hit your spirit like a middle linebacker, you'll never mistake them for the confusing words of the Enemy. When the spirit of God's voice rains down hope on your soul, you'll learn to reject the whispers of shame that well up from your sinful nature. After hearing the guiding principles of God's Word, the Enemy's attempts to destroy you will become clear. It will all become clear. God wants it that way. The entire history of His faithful listeners declares it so.

> He calls his own sheep by name and leads them out. When he has brought out all his own, he goes on ahead of them, and his sheep follow him because they know his voice. But they will never follow a stranger; in fact, they will run away from him because they do not recognize a stranger's voice. (John 10:3-5)

Do you need to lay down any misconceptions about the way God speaks? Have you mistaken a different voice for God's? Pray today for discernment. Ask the Spirit to teach you to recognize God's voice. Give Him daily opportunities to develop your ear for Christ.

DAY FIVE

Tune In

The fifth day of each week is an opportunity to dig in to God's Word and spend time in prayer and worship. It's a chance to assimilate all you've discovered during the week.

George Muller put it well:

> It often astonished me that I did not see the importance of meditation upon Scripture earlier in my Christian life. As the outward man is not fit for work for any length of time unless he eats, so it is with the inner man. What is the food for the inner man? Not prayer, but *the Word of God*—not the simple reading of the Word of God, so that it only passes through our minds, just as water runs through a pipe. No, we must consider what we read, ponder over it, and apply it to our hearts.[7]

Take this time each week, Girls. God is not impressed with a completed workbook or filled-in blanks. He wants your heart. Use this opportunity to spend time with the Spirit as He teaches you to hear His voice. There is no way to discover it outside of time spent in the Word of God.

Before you begin, ask the Holy Spirit to enrich your time and multiply His Word to you. Pray for clarity and understanding.

Turn to Matthew 13:1-23, and read straight through. Then go back and work through each section as outlined below. After each part, spend time reading, pondering, praying, and journaling. Regardless of how you feel about journaling, it focuses your attention and allows you to process, so whether you use bullet points, fragmented sentences, or write like C.S. Lewis, put your pen to paper.

Feel free to use any of the prompts—not all of them. This is not a list of questions to answer, just some suggestions on responding to this passage. If you take one suggestion and go off on a tangent, so be it. Or allow the Spirit to lead you however He sees fit.

Verses 1-9: This is a story Jesus told about listening to God. The seed is His word, and we represent the various soils as listeners.

- Why do you think Jesus said what He did in verse 9? Of course everyone had ears. What do you think He was getting at?

Verses 10-17:

- Who do you think Jesus was talking about here? What do you think He meant by "though hearing, they do not hear"? Do you relate to this? Have you ever?
- Do you gather that these unhearing people have no hope of ever understanding His words? What did Jesus say about that? What does that tell you about Him? If you don't hear Him clearly at this point, how do these verses affect you?

- What does hearing and understanding His voice seem to be a function of?

Verses 18-19:

- What kind of person do you think this is? Practically speaking, how would this person receive the words of God? What attitudes might you see?
- Why do you think they "don't understand"? What role does the Evil One play? Do you think the Enemy is solely responsible, or is this a joint effort?
- Is this you? Do you feel like nothing has ever been sown in your heart? Are you a path with no soil for God's Word? Allow your heart to be searched by "the candle of the Lord."

Verses 20-21:

- What kind of listener do you think this is? Why does she have no root? How does that become the reality for a believer?
- Given the fallout, what do you think she *expected* to hear from God?
- What sorts of emotions toward God would you guess she experienced as she fell away? How might she characterize God's presence after the carnage? What attitude do you see in this type of fallen believer?
- Believer, is this you? Did you want His voice to bring only happiness and promptly deliver your requests? Have trials damaged your untested faith? Honestly journal through your experience. Don't forget to take notice of your roots in Christ. How deep were they dug?

Verse 22:

- Who is this? How did God's words fall on this believer?
  Why?
- What do you think this believer had hoped to hear
  from God? Does that explain her fall?
- What are those thorns? What are they in your life?
  How do you allow them to choke out God's voice?
  Why did Jesus call this person "unfruitful"?
- Does this ring familiar? Have worries or the pursuit
  of wealth suffocated God's voice to you? Do you bear
  no fruit for Christ? Spend some time here allowing
  the Spirit to show you the thorns that keep you from
  growing strong.

Verse 23:

- Here is the listener God wants. Why do you think Jesus
  called this person "good soil"? How does that apply to
  hearing His voice?
- What does this type of believer's life look like? What
  does she expect to hear from God? More importantly,
  how does she respond? What can God do with this
  listener?
- How does this relate to verses 11-12?

Believer, Jesus rarely explained His parables, yet He saw
fit to interpret this one for us. Doesn't that seem significant?
Perhaps He anticipated the gigantic "I can't hear God's voice"
objection, so He made it evident that His voice is clear; it's our
ears that pose the problem. He referred to "hearing" ten times
in this short passage. You alone are responsible for the soil of
your heart. God's Word was delivered identically, but the seed
was only planted in the heart of the *listener*.

Will you be this last listener? Will you dig deep roots through discipleship and enable the Word to stick? Will you prune those thorns? Will you receive God's Word no matter what it is? Will your faith produce a crop rather than unfruitfulness? Offer your willingness to God today. With His help, lay aside any hindrance that has kept His voice at bay. There is hope for every believer who is willing.

"They might see with their eyes, hear with their ears, understand with their hearts and turn, and I would heal them." (Matthew 13:15)

He Speaks Through Disciplines

[JESUS]

God's Word.

My mother-in-law, Jacki, loves to tell stories about my husband, and I in turn love to hear them, as they provide excellent teasing opportunities. He gets plenty of fodder at my house, too, as my family happily recounts "Jen: The Awkward Years." It's a big toss-up as to which of us was the bigger dork. I'm the reigning champ in the Third Through Sixth Grade category, and Brandon edged me out in the Eighth Through Eleventh Grade category.

Jacki tells how Brandon would go missing when he was little. Early on, this threw her into panic mode, and she'd go on a psychotic tear looking for her more-than-likely abducted child. But soon Jacki discovered that Brandon was always in the same place. She'd casually walk into the kitchen, open the bottom cabinet, and there Brandon would be sitting with a saucepan on his head. I have the pictures to prove it, so help me. When she couldn't find him, she knew just where to look.

Together we're going to study twenty ways God speaks to us, but it cannot be stressed enough that the permanent address of God's voice is His Word. It should *always* be the first place we go. God speaks loud and clear within the pages of

Scripture. A suffering friend told me angrily, "I can't hear God saying anything to me. He's giving me nothing. He's nowhere." I had to ask, "What is He telling you in the Word?" Her eyes dropped and she answered, "I haven't really been there."

Well, my stars! There are over 774,000 words in there! God worked hard to get His words recorded so we could hang on every one of them. His written Word transcended culture, distance, and persecution as He protected it. He pulled together forty-plus writers over 1,500 years and inspired them through the Holy Spirit, even before He was universally available. Supernaturally, they all agreed on mega-themes of truth, though most had no opportunity to collaborate. And He's not saying anything to us? I'm positive God gets chest pains when He hears that.

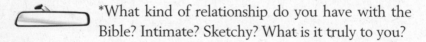 *What kind of relationship do you have with the Bible? Intimate? Sketchy? What is it truly to you?

This will be evidenced by how much time you spend there. When does Bible study fit in your life? Once a week? Daily? Never? Why?

As we look to God's primary mode of communication, let's turn an eye to the Living Word: Jesus. John the Baptist, Jesus' relative, announced Jesus' coming ministry. John's role was prophesied long before he walked this earth, not unlike Jesus.

John was a special cat, and he had amazing parents: his father was a priest, his mother also from a priestly family. John was born to them under extraordinary circumstances (next week's treasure), as they were well advanced in years with no previous children. His birth had angels, incense, miracles, prophecy (see Luke 1). I'm just saying John was a serious player. He was born into spiritual greatness.

John's adult ministry was so powerful, people constantly

wondered if he was the promised Messiah. Yet with no excep-
tions, John pointed them to Jesus saying, "I baptize you with
water. But one more powerful than I will come, the thongs of
whose sandals I am not worthy to untie. He will baptize you
with the Holy Spirit and with fire" (3:16).

As God had said all along, John's ministry was as a forerunner to Jesus. It was a message of preparation. The role of co-
laborers with Jesus had been appointed to others. No sooner
did Jesus go public with His own ministry than Herod threw
John into prison for rebuking his adulterous marriage (see
3:19-20). Perhaps knowing his time was near, John communicated one last time with Jesus through two of his disciples
who visited him in prison.

Read Luke 7:18-20. Wow. What emotions do you think
John was experiencing to send this message? What
might he have been thinking?

*Given their unique relationship, what would you think Jesus'
response might have been?

Before we cast any stones, remember that for all the build
up—his entire life basically—John never saw Jesus' ministry come to fruition. He spent thirty years preparing others
for what he barely had the chance to witness. Here in Jesus'
first public year, our Savior hadn't made a big splash yet.
Jesus hadn't attracted much attention from His followers or
His enemies. What's more, John was captive in a dungeon at
Machaerus, "The Black Fortress," that Herod the Great built
on the east side of the Jordan where no one went.[1]

Sweet Jesus. No hint of disappointment in John's question.
Instead, Jesus delivered the most reassuring message to John.
A simple yes was not sufficient for the state His friend was in.

🔊 Read Luke 7:21-23. Why do you think Jesus answered like this?

As the son of a priest, John was well-educated in Scripture, which was just the Old Testament at that time. He knew the Word backward and forward. In fact, he used it liberally in his teachings. In the few New Testament passages that recount John's ministry, he demonstrated an advanced knowledge of biblical prophecy. As he *was* a prophet, let's just call that redundant. Jesus communicated something special to John that day:

- Luke 7:22: "Go back and report to John what you have seen and heard: The blind receive sight, the lame walk, those who have leprosy are cured, the deaf hear." Compare a prophecy about the Messiah from 700 years earlier: "Then will the eyes of the blind be opened and the ears of the deaf unstopped. Then will the lame leap like a deer" (Isaiah 35:5-6).
- Luke 7:22: "The dead are raised, and the good news is preached to the poor." Compare Isaiah 61:1: "The Spirit of the Sovereign LORD is on me, because the LORD has anointed me to preach good news to the poor."

🔊 How do you think Jesus' use of Scripture affected John's faith?

So what about Jesus? Did He send that confirmation to John but secretly shake His head at the question? We often expect that reaction when we need assurance. We hesitate to ask because we should know better. Surely questions like that annoy Jesus and expose our weaknesses. He has the whole world to manage, and we're asking if He really loves us again. Bad, bad. Right?

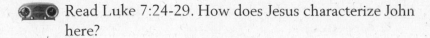 Read Luke 7:24-29. How does Jesus characterize John here?

And guess what strategy Jesus used again as He spurred on those new believers? He referenced familiar biblical prophecy from four centuries earlier: "'See, I will send my messenger, who will prepare the way before me. Then suddenly the Lord you are seeking will come to his temple; the messenger of the covenant, whom you desire, will come,' says the LORD Almighty" (Malachi 3:1). Sound familiar? It did to those Jews, too. They spent their entire childhoods studying Scripture.

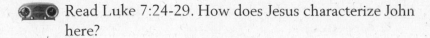 How did Jesus' use of the Word affect their faith?

But Jesus said, "Yet the one who is least in the kingdom of God is greater than he" (verse 28). Oh Girls, John announced salvation through grace, but we have it. As Matthew Henry put it: "The meanest of those that *follow* the Lamb far excel the greatest of those that went *before* him."[2] We have the Word completed, save for Jesus' final return. We have the fulfilled Scriptures written in English with red letters and footnotes and cross references and indexes and concordances. We have it online in every translation. We have every resource to help us unpack it. We have the Holy Spirit to bring it to life. Jesus was right on.

Through Scripture, Jesus told John, "I am the One. Your faith has been well placed. Your ministry is perfectly fulfilled. Blessed are you, friend of the Bridegroom." Peace in the end when he needed it most. Through it, Jesus explained to the new converts, "God chose John long ago. The message he gave you is true. Your baptism by him is received with joy." The hope of salvation confirmed. Through it, He has spoken life to millions of believers:

"You are redeemed."

"I am faithful."

"Grace cannot be earned. It is My gift to you."

"You are My handiwork."

"Nothing is beyond My reach."

 *What is the clearest message you ever heard through the Bible?

God will speak to you there. It's a forgone conclusion. There is no question of "Will He speak?" through it. It is a question of "Will you give Him the chance to?" The Bible is not an antiquated collection of really old stories. "The word of God is living and active. Sharper than any double-edged sword, it penetrates even to dividing soul and spirit" (Hebrews 4:12). It has the power to speak to *your* circumstances, to transform *your* soul. Your job is to open it. There are over 774,000 of God's words in there.

Some of them are bound to be for you.

Do you give God a fighting chance to speak to you through the Word? How much time do you give Him? Ask God to shine His light on this area in your life. Pray for specifics on what needs to change. Offer Him consistent time in the Bible to change your life.

Prayer

*I*t's probably the singular reason I married so young (other than my irresistible beau, naturally): I hated dating. I couldn't figure it out. I could never tactfully hold my tongue, and that proved unfortunate more than once. I wore my emotions on my sleeve and never mastered "mysteriously sexy" according to *Seventeen* magazine, circa 1988.

Worse than my own deficiencies were those of the future felons I dated. Hands down, the worst part about dating losers was the actual dates. I'd try with every fiber within to facilitate conversation, and my date sat there like a deaf mute. Four, five-word answers maybe. No interest in asking me anything. Apparently, no interest in answering either. The tension was enough to send me into a coma—which I would have welcomed.

As we engage the voice of God, we cannot go another step without addressing prayer. Because what is prayer if not a two-way conversation? It's that horrific date where evidently only one party has the power of speech. You might feel like you're talking, begging, rambling on but receiving nothing back. Believer, God can talk, too. In fact, it may be that He is trying to get your attention, but you've checked out. If prayer is not a dialogue, Jesus has some thoughts for you. Let's dig in.

As our ultimate model, Jesus was a man of prayer. No doubt about it:

> But Jesus often withdrew to lonely places and prayed. (Luke 5:16)

> One of those days Jesus went out to a mountainside to pray, and spent the night praying to God. (6:12)

> About eight days after Jesus said this, he took Peter, John and James with him and went up onto a mountain to pray. (9:28)

Girls, Jesus had no spiritual need to be baptized, yet He did it. He was too glorious to wash His disciples' feet, but He stooped to do so. Likewise, Jesus was one with God; His knowledge was complete—past, present, and future. He knew a level of inner contact with His Father that you and I can never fully experience. The apostle John said of Jesus: "In the beginning was the Word, and the Word was with God, and *the Word was God*" (John 1:1). Jesus' life was a living prayer: unhindered communion, constant communication.

*So why do you think Jesus withdrew so often to pray? List every reason you can think of.

Biblically, prayer is presented as a proven format between God and mankind. There is no question of "Will God speak through prayer?" That He *will* speak underlies the whole point of it. The question is: "Am I allowing Him to speak to me through prayer?" Not only did Jesus lead by example, but He delivered some brilliant teaching on prayer to show us how.

Read Matthew 6:5-6. Have you ever been guilty of praying to be seen? How about making a noisy display of a "prayer request" with no plans to actually pray about it? Describe your experience.

This is not an indictment against all public praying or sharing. Jesus was going to a heart issue. Religion is so often bartered for attention. It is leveraged for sympathy, sometimes for esteem. Prayer can be put on like a garish costume to draw the notice of others. This wasn't just done on the street corners in first-century Galilee. It's done from pulpits, in small groups, among friends, on television. There is prayer from a sincere heart, and there is everything else. The first is effective; the second is offensive. Jesus made it crystal clear: The attention they receive is "their reward in full." Those prayers are neither regarded nor answered. Talk about a one-way conversation.

Read Matthew 6:7-8. Why is God opposed to this sort of thing?

The *New American Standard Bible* calls these prayers "meaningless repetitions." This includes wordy phraseology designed to impress the listeners. I kid you not, I once heard a pastor exclaim in prayer, "Oh, blessed Lord of the Harvest! You are thrice holy!" My sisters and I dissolved in laughter, and I couldn't recover for the rest of the service. I'd like to tell you I was sixteen, but this was last year. Who says that? Is "thrice" even a word? Was that declared to worship God or to sound pretty? I'll go to the grave saying it did neither.

But I've been guilty of this, too. Now I've never said "thrice" to God for fear He would laugh out loud at me, but I have given thoughtless offerings of churchy clichés and careless declarations plenty of times. I've also been so preoccupied with making my prayer sound right, I've disengaged my mind from the God I was praying to. Worthless! In fact, Jesus said, "They *think* they will be heard." Ouch.

 *Have meaningless repetitions or worthless words affected your prayer life? If so, how?

So after these prayer-busters, Jesus showed us what to do. I spoke to a new believer recently who asked, "Is there some-place in the Bible that shows me how to pray? I don't know what I'm doing." Listen, I've been at this most of my life, but when I pray so long my study group starts nodding off, I clearly demonstrate that sometimes I don't know what I'm doing either. Let's learn from Jesus together.

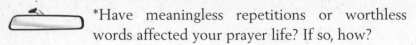 Read Matthew 6:9-13. Sum up the focus of each verse in a word or phrase.

Verse 9

Verse 10

Verse 11

Verse 12

Verse 13

What a beautiful model! It probably took Jesus fifteen seconds to say that, yet every subject was covered. He always chose the simple over the complicated. No hint of pomp and circumstance. No flowery wording fit for a plaque. And as only Jesus could, He demonstrated a prayer that can grow with the maturity of the pray-er. As James Orr noted, "For those who are not able to bring their struggling desires to birth in articu-late language, it provides an instructive form. To the mature disciple, it ever unfolds with richer depths of meaning."[3]

Jesus demonstrated balance: This wasn't a one-sided prayer to grant our desires. It wasn't just a laborious rehashing of our sins. It wasn't only a fearful reflection on God's greatness. Rather it involved a progressive, balanced discussion. What else is there? Each element belongs just where Jesus placed it.

*Do your prayers tend to get out of balance? If so, what do you overemphasize and underemphasize? Why do you think that is?

So after you've offered pure prayers from sincere motives, don't forget to listen. Most of us pray like we're leaving a voicemail message, not having a conversation. If we never take a breath during a prayer, then run off to tend to business, when would God have the chance to speak?

In his book *The Secret of Guidance*, Frederick B. Meyer gave some practical advice: "Be still each day for a short time, sitting before God in meditation, and ask the Holy Spirit to reveal to you the truth of Christ's indwelling. Ask God *to be pleased* to make known to you what is the riches of the glory of this mystery (Colossians 1:27)."[4] I love that. To cultivate a consistent spirit of listening will do wonders for your communication with God. Sometimes He will speak to you instantly. Sometimes He will allow you to rest in His presence while He reserves His words for later. Either way, you are listening, so you will hear from your Father.

As Dallas Willard so aptly noted of God:

He is not frivolous or coy; he will not tease or torture us. In our relationship with him there is no mysterious catch to receiving his word for us, no riddle to solve, no incantation to get just right—not with the God and Father of our Lord Jesus Christ! We must make a point of not thinking of him in terms of human beings (relatives, supervisors, authorities and others) who may have enjoyed tricking us by not explaining what we were supposed to do.[5]

How good are you at sitting in silence? Why is that?

Oh, Girls, I've rarely experienced sweeter moments than sitting quietly at God's feet. When my daughter had her first seizure at age four, we spent an excruciating night in the ER as she endured procedures I couldn't have managed. After watching her suffer and fearing her diagnosis, we finally came home. Her daddy slept on the floor next to her all night. I went to my bed alone, and wracking sobs that had been held at bay made me almost sick. In my distress, I was so terrified for her I couldn't even pray words. I could only drag myself into God's presence and weep.

In the silence, God spoke as clearly as if He was sitting next to me: "Go on and cry, Dear One. I know what it's like to fear for your child. You don't need to say anything. The Holy Spirit is hovered over you praying on your behalf." Comfort. Security. Loud and clear.

That is my God.

When you ask with pure motives jealous for the will of God, it is given. When you seek to know the Father to the father-less, you will find Him. When you humbly knock on the door of heaven, it will be opened. To be in His presence, to pray in meekness, is to allow God's voice to wash over you. It is His will. It is His way. It is His desire.

"Call to me and I will answer you." (Jeremiah 33:3)

Has the quality of your prayers rendered God's voice silent? Are they selfish? Agenda-driven? Unengaged? Non-existent? Have you forgotten to listen? Ask God to reveal your prayer life clearly today. Ask Him to show you if anything is keeping His voice from you. Commit to a daily time to pray simply and sit quietly.

Fasting

God often is the initiator of conversation with His children. He has spoken to me while I was making a peanut butter sandwich, driving on the highway listening to U2, awakened at 4 a.m., and countless other times when His voice literally came out of left field. If I didn't think it would hurt God's feelings, I'd call those experiences spooky.

But there are times when we desperately need God's voice, and we initiate the conversation. Those times go beyond daily prayer into a different realm, a realm of intensity and urgency. It's that place where we cannot lift our heads without a word from God. We become like David when he begged:

> To you I call, O Lord my Rock;
>   do not turn a deaf ear to me.
> For if you remain silent,
>   I will be like those who have gone down to the pit.
> Hear my cry for mercy
>   as I call to you for help,
> as I lift up my hands
>   toward your Most Holy Place. (Psalm 28:1-2)

God gave us a wonderful, misunderstood, amazing method of tapping into His voice when we find ourselves in this desperate place: fasting.

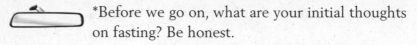 *Before we go on, what are your initial thoughts on fasting? Be honest.

Fasting is a curious discipline to modern believers. Of course, the Israelites fasted as a common practice. It was on par with prayer or worship. But for some reason we've eliminated fasting from our spiritual diets (lame pun). Probably the notion of sacrifice—or more accurately, hunger—scares us off. Maybe it's a lack of understanding. Perhaps it's the absence of role models to learn from. Any way you slice it, fasting is a lost practice, yet it's a certain way to communicate with God.

There is so much gobbledygook out there on fasting, it's staggering. As I researched, I'm pretty sure I lost four days somewhere. Tons of people pontificate on fasting, from how long it "must" be, to when, to how, to blah, blah, blah. So rather than latch onto someone's opinion (which is possibly how fasting got so misdirected), let's go to the Word.

Why Fast?

According to God's Word, fasting was either commanded or initiated during one of six extreme circumstances:

- Mourning
- Inquiry
- Repentance
- Preparation
- Crisis
- Communion/Worship

Have you ever desperately needed a word from God in one of these areas? When?

Read Isaiah 58:6-7. What sorts of things does God want to accomplish through a healthy fast?

*How is this different from dieting or skipping a meal?

Read Isaiah 58:8-9. Wow. What connections do you see between these results and the six reasons for a fast listed earlier?

Girls, these are the treasures of heaven. Freedom realized. Ministry accomplished. A fast from food creates emptiness, space for God to move like this. So often the clutter and routine and monotony of our lives crowd out this depth of communion. To temporarily change our routine of comfort is to jar us off high-center. It ushers in a fresh awareness of God. It is not necessarily something we offer Him, but rather it assists us in offering ourselves. As Bill Bright, founder of Campus Crusade for Christ, said, "It is exchanging the needs of the physical body for those of the spirit."[6]

Today, fasting is often snubbed because we obsess about the hunger, the logistics, the mechanics, and we become frozen. God is about the communion, the results. The fast is simply the means to a wonderful end, but we don't see that as plainly. It is a divine opportunity to commune with God at a depth most of us have never experienced. I'm not making that up. That's exactly what God is saying in Isaiah. He obviously knows something about fasting that we have misunderstood. Yet, there are some boundaries God outlined in a little piece I'm calling. . . .

"Don't Bother"

Seeking God's voice with poor motives or a disobedient heart is about as effective as reasoning with a two-year-old. God cuts through junk like a laser. He is not impressed with our empty sacrifices. Our hunger pains do not compel Him to move if our hearts are wrong. Might as well eat a big burger and be done with it.

Read God's thoughts on an insincere fast in Isaiah 58:1-5. Why did Israel's fasting offend God?

If any one thing becomes clear to you over the course of this study, I hope it is this: Hearing God's voice is only possible in the life of an obedient disciple. The end. We simply cannot manipulate God to speak His treasures when it suits us while ignoring everything else He says.

Can you hear His distress in this passage? We've seen what He wants to accomplish through a fast, and it's a beautiful work. Yet His people came in selfishness and disobedience and cried, "Why have we fasted and you have not seen it?" They thought they were being obedient with their religiosity, yet they missed the entire point. Don't you know God wanted to pull His hair out?

It wasn't for lack of desire to hear Him. As God observed, "They ask me for just decisions and seem eager for God to come near them." No doubt there are times we truly want to hear from Him, but it's all the *other* moments of our lives that dictate how much He will or will not be saying.

How Long?

So what is up with fasting? Does God have a certain way to do it? An exact time frame? Actually, outside the heart of the believer, specifics on fasting are sparse in Scripture. With pure motives and humility, God flooded His listeners with more communion than they could handle. God has always been compelled by sincerity.

Originally, only one day of fasting was required in the law, on the Day of Atonement. By the end of the Old Testament period, three other days had been added throughout the course of a year. Each fast was one day long.

Outside those required fasts, others were initiated on a need basis. They were recorded as one day, three days, seven days, several days, twenty-one days, and the longest at forty days, which Jesus went through. When done in obedience, God responded to them all, so His history declares that He does not have a magic number.

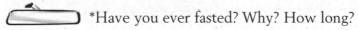 *Have you ever fasted? Why? How long?

How did God speak to you through it?

I've fasted a few times, but a close examination of God's Word tells me that I have missed some critical opportunities. I have thus far fasted under the "inquiry" banner. Not "What should I make for dinner?" but "What should I do with my life?" kinds of inquiries. God spoke every time.

But Girls, I've never been so distressed over my own sin that I fasted in repentance. I haven't fasted before God when mourning threatened to overtake me. And though it now seems ridiculous, I didn't fast in preparation for the ministry God called me to. Not that I didn't spend hours on my knees in prayer, but fasting is God's special tool for urgency.

*Do you have a need for God's voice on this level right now? If so, what is it?

If God ordained fasting from the beginning of Scripture,

don't you think He had good grounds? After all, Jesus said, *"When* you fast" (Matthew 6:16), not *"If* you fast." He doesn't waste our time. Fasting goes well beyond self-denial, as some boil it down to. For divine reasons, the inward space it creates allows God to communicate with special depth, focused intimacy.

Jesus delivered more powerful teaching on the heart of fasting (Matthew 6:16-18), but I bet most of us aren't fasting poorly. I suspect we're not fasting at all. If, in our most desperate moments, God gave us a format for laying aside self and being freed by His very hand, why wouldn't we jump at the chance?

> "Even now," declares the LORD,
>> "return to me with all your heart,
>> with fasting and weeping and mourning."
> Rend your heart
>> and not your garments.
> Return to the LORD your God,
>> for he is gracious and compassionate,
>> slow to anger and abounding in love. (Joel 2:12-13)

Do you need to reconsider fasting in your life? Is God calling you to one now? Ask Him for guidance and revelation toward this discipline. Be willing to be obedient. You can do anything through Him who gives you strength.

Some helpful websites that further detail fasting are:

1. http://www.freedomyou.com/fasting_book/
   Fasting Tips.htm
2. http://www.billbright.com/howtofast/
3. http://www.livingwd.org/ministries/prayers/
   fastingandprayer.asp

Worship

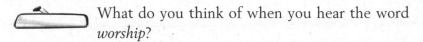 What do you think of when you hear the word *worship?*

I fear we've made a mess of worship these days. We've diluted it to such an anemic condition that it has become a line item on our spiritual list. Perhaps we equate it to singing (provided the music suits our liking). Or it's a chance to assuage our guilt from the rest of the week when we *weren't* worshiping. We often think of it as an experience, a specific block of time, and evaluate it not by God's pleasure but by what we did—or did not—receive.

Girls, go with me today to the depths of worship. Let's take a closer look at the way God established it and how Jesus revolutionized it.

If there was ever doubt about how serious God was about worship, one need only read the Old Testament dissertation on the temple, its components, and the sacrifices required. You'll need three cups of coffee before you can effectively dive in there. Let me tell you something: God was not playing around. He painted a picture of His extreme holiness and the

Israelites' extreme unworthiness to worship in His presence. Bringing the two together was like mixing oil and water.

God's very presence was housed in the ark of the covenant, kept behind a large curtain in the Holy of Holies, the innermost sanctuary of the temple. (Your Bible may have a diagram of the temple floor plan.) Only the high priest—and only once a year on the required day of fasting—could enter to offer a sacrifice of atonement for the nation's sins. And don't think that was a simple matter of shoving the curtain aside and sprinkling a little blood around. This sacrifice, this worship, was so sacred that God gave at least one hundred directives on how it had to be done.

In fact, in case one item was out of place, God commanded of the hem of the high priest's robe: "Make pomegranates of blue, purple and scarlet yarn around the hem of the robe, with *gold bells* between them. . . . Aaron must wear it when he ministers. The sound of the bells will be heard when he enters the Holy Place before the LORD and when he comes out, so that he will not die" (Exodus 28:33,35). In other words, if the worship was tainted, the high priest would be struck dead instantly, and the other priests would know by the silence of the bells. According to Jewish tradition, they would then pull him out by a rope tied around his ankle. Yikes.

*What do you think God was communicating about worship?

And lest I paint a picture of a once-a-year God, He also established daily offerings to be continually brought before Him in worship. Read Exodus 29:38-46. What did these daily offerings secure for the Israelites?

Let's be clear: Had the priests approached worship the way many of us do, they would have rendered themselves extinct. God is holy. So very holy. We have no concept of how holy and perfect He is. That God could even be close to sinful mankind is stunning, which is why it was so complicated to bring worship that wouldn't offend His perfection.

He is *still* that holy.

Which brings us back to Jesus.

Though some 1,400 years passed after the original tabernacle was instituted, the Holy Place in the temple remained identical in Jesus' day. In 19 BC, Herod the Great began construction of the new temple in Jerusalem to ingratiate himself to his hostile Jewish constituents. It was a grand affair. He built it around the old temple in excessive white marble stones with heavy gold overlay. He hung elaborate tapestries and enlarged the outer courts. It was said that there was so much gold covering the building that no one could look directly at it in bright sunlight.[7] This was the temple Jesus knew.

However, at age twelve, Jesus could already see through the grandeur of the temple enough to call it "my Father's house" (Luke 2:49). Herod might have changed its façade, but Jesus would forever change its significance. Though most of His ministry took place in Galilee, Jesus traveled to this temple in Jerusalem every year for Passover, as was the custom. We have several accounts of His teaching and healing in the temple courts while He was there to worship each year.

But in Jesus' final week, He spent almost all His time in the Jerusalem temple. Because they inform modern worship, let's look briefly at the principles Jesus preserved within the temple gates that last week.

Read the following passages and jot down the basic standards Jesus emphasized concerning worship in His Father's house:

Monday in the temple: Mark 11:15-17

Tuesday in the temple:

Mark 12:28-34

Mark 12:38-40

Mark 12:41-44

*Do you see any of these principles of worship distorted today in His Father's house? How so?

But the best for last: Though it pains us to read about Jesus' crucifixion, it was truly His finest hour. As Isaiah so perfectly prophesied:

We considered him stricken by God,
    smitten by him, and afflicted.
But he was pierced for our transgressions,
    he was crushed for our iniquities;
the punishment that brought us peace was upon him,
    and by his wounds we are healed. (Isaiah 53:4-5)

Oh, are we ever healed.

Read of the moment Jesus died on the cross in Mark 15:37-38. How did Jesus' sacrifice forever change worship from how it had been since its inception?

Believer, the temple originally declared that worship from sinful man to a holy God was terribly expensive, entirely sacred. He provided an initial means to bridge the gap through the blood of lambs, goats, bulls, and rams; incense, altars, oil, and lamps; robes, ephods, breastpieces, and bells. Yet, as the writer of Hebrews explained, the blood of animals could not take away sins permanently nor usher all of mankind into

God's presence (see 10:4). They were only checks that would ultimately have to be covered by blood in the bank account of the True Lamb of God, Jesus Christ. He became both the high priest and the sacrificial lamb to render the original covenant obsolete.

*Here it is! Read Hebrews 10:19-23. How does God want you to worship now?

There is hardly a sweeter verse than this: "God's temple is sacred, and *you* are that temple" (1 Corinthians 3:17). Sweet Girls, we have been ushered into the Holy Place by the sacrifice of our Savior. We can stand there with confidence, but it is still a holy place.

Your life is that Holy Place.

A place of worship and purity, sacrifice, and glory. A place of daily offerings and praise. Jesus changed its location, not its sanctity. Just because worship became more accessible does not make it less sacred. Our freedom was never meant to become our complacency. Girls, our lives should be a continuous reflection of worship, just as the Holy Place was when it was first established.

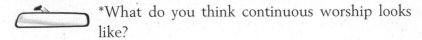 *What do you think continuous worship looks like?

What, if anything, needs to change in your daily life in order to offer this kind of worship?

Wondering what on earth this has to do with hearing God? Let me remind you of God's original purpose for worship in the Holy Place:

"*There* I will meet you and speak to you" (Exodus 29:42).

When the animals had been prepared for sacrifice, the garments were donned, and the oil was sprinkled, God spoke.

When the lambs were offered daily at twilight and dawn, God spoke. When the lamps were lit with fragrant incense around the clock, God spoke. When the high priest made blood atonement on the horns of the altar each year, God spoke.

How else could His voice have been so clear to His people in the Old Testament? Their obedience to God's explicit terms of reverence kept His voice active. Scripture confirms this, both from God's leadership in seasons of obedience as well as its absence when Israel failed to worship. The latter was the case when Samuel first came on the scene during a dark period of rebellion: "The boy Samuel ministered before the LORD under Eli. In those days the word of the LORD was rare; there were not many visions" (1 Samuel 3:1).

 Do you see a link between your life as worship and God's voice to you? How so?

Your life is the Holy Place, Believer. Not a place to be selfish or careless. Not a place to fulfill its purpose a few minutes a week. As true worshipers, the dailiness of our lives should reflect adoration, reverence, and sacrifice. Worship is not encapsulated in a moment or a singular experience. In the constant presence of God—paid for with the priceless blood of Christ—let's long to obey His original desire: "There shall be *perpetual* incense before the LORD throughout your generations" (Exodus 30:8, NASB).

May your lamp of worship constantly burn.

There, He will meet you and speak to you.

Does your life worship God? Could His voice be silent because of the absence of reverence? Ask God to reveal any ways in which you have distorted worship. Pray for perpetual incense to burn in your heart, the Holy Place.

Tune In

Girls, let's spend some time with Jesus today as He perfectly modeled all four disciplines in one spectacular passage. As you read through each section, pray and meditate on God's truth. Feel free to use any of the prompts or allow the Spirit to lead you differently as you journal today. Remember, this is not a list of questions to answer; they are simply provided to demonstrate a healthy interaction with Scripture. Productive Bible study is all about asking good questions.

Ask God to enlarge your boundaries. Pray for illumination to light the path you're on and the path ahead in these areas. Read Matthew 4:1-11 straight through, then go back through each of the following sections.

Read Matthew 4:1-2. This took place just after John baptized Jesus and just before the launch of His public ministry.

- Given that information, why do you think the Spirit "led" Jesus to a forty-day fast? What does this tell you about fasting?

- Why might God have chosen a desert for this experience?
- During forty days of fasting, Jesus was tempted by Satan. How would you guess Satan might tempt a believer engaged in a Spirit-led fast?

Read Matthew 4:3-4.

- Out of the three recorded temptations, why do you think Satan went here first? What does that tell you about the Enemy?
- Jesus quoted Deuteronomy 8:3, a passage about the time when Moses and the Israelites had been wandering in the desert for almost forty years before entering the Promised Land. Read Deuteronomy 8:1-9. What comparisons do you see between that account and Jesus' fast?
- What does this passage in Matthew communicate about God's Word? Has Scripture ever delivered you like this? When have you said, "It is written: . . ."?

Read Matthew 4:5-7.

- Why do you think Satan took Jesus to His "Father's house" in Jerusalem?
- Satan also quoted Scripture—Psalm 91:11-12. Has the Enemy ever distorted Scripture to use against you? How so?
- What does Jesus' answer teach you about studying God's Word?
- Are you ready for battle? Are you armed with the Word of Truth? Ask God to reveal the gaps in your armor and

show you how He wants Bible study to intersect your daily life.

Read Matthew 4:8-11.

- How did Satan package false worship? What did he offer to sweeten the pot? How does he still do this today?
- It's interesting that even with the acquisition of all these things, Jesus still had to bow down. Have you been deceived? Do you feel like you are bowing to no one, not God or the Enemy? Read Matthew 12:30 and ask Jesus to show you the truth of His words.
- How are you tempted away from the worship of God? What does the Enemy offer you?
- How does continual worship prepare you for these moments of temptation rather than occasional worship?

Jesus fasted in preparation for three arduous years of ministry that would end in torture. No doubt He spent forty days in fervent prayer—no distractions in a barren desert. Years of studying the Word prepared Him even as He was weak from hunger and isolation. His worship was reserved for His Father, even though Satan offered Him many appealing prizes if He would share it.

"Then the devil left him, and angels came and attended him." They must have wanted to minister to their King sooner; after all, with one call twelve legions of angels would have been at Jesus' disposal (see Matthew 26:53). Yet God allowed the Word and Spirit—intensified by fasting and prayer—to work their power in Jesus' temptation. And they were sufficient.

They will be for you, too.

Do you really want to hear God? You could stop right here and have enough communication to fill your ears for a lifetime. Offer God your time, your worship. Dig into His Word—it's a treasure trove. Talk to Him every single day. Listen to Him, too. If God leads you, consider a fast. Girls, these are the proven connections to heaven. Pray for new resolve to listen through these disciplines.

He Speaks Through People

(MARY AND JOSEPH)

His Image

I recently picked up my three-year-old from morning preschool. Now understand that he is a pistol, a man-child whose humor has single-handedly saved him from certain destruction. Quite frankly, he does what he wants. He lives in Caleb World on Caleb Time, and the rest of us accommodate his demands because, honestly, we're a little scared of him.

He eagerly pointed out their art project for the morning: a bird made out of a paper plate, feathers, and googly eyes. I glanced at the display, taking in the appropriate work of the other kids: two eyes just above the beak, feathers glued to the sides, legs on the bottom. Adorable.

Then I spotted Caleb's.

There was really no mistaking it. His bird had three eyes not by the beak (as his had no beak), but just next to its pooper. The feathers were glued helter-skelter, making it look like an accessory Joan Crawford might put on her head. The two legs were sticking out from the front of the bird—toes inward—as if it had been skewered by renegade forks. With a smile, Caleb said, "That's mine."

As if anyone thought it wasn't.

It's amazing what you can learn about someone by looking at what he has created. Volumes are communicated about his personality and passion simply through the handiwork of the artist. His work declares, "This is who I am."

Of His people, God proclaimed:

"They are the shoot I have planted,
   the work of my hands,
   for the display of my splendor." (Isaiah 60:21)

We're going to look closely this week at what God has communicated through His handiwork. By deliberate design, He has spoken of Himself and of mankind in staggering clarity. Much of this communication has been distorted, yet it stands as the foundation of our relationship with a Holy God. Let's begin at the beginning.

Read Genesis 1:26. After six-and-a-half days of creating the rest of the world, God announced His crowning work. Up until this moment, God spoke matter-of-factly: "Let there be light." "Let there be land." And there was. Yet on the sixth day, God turned to the other members of His heavenly Trinity, and said, "Let us make man in our image." *Let there be* turned into *let us make*. An excited conversation, a shared passion; they stood on the cusp of realizing God's vision for all of existence. Matthew Henry wrote, "It should seem as if this were the work which he longed to be at; as if he had said, 'Having at last settled the preliminaries, let us now apply ourselves to the business, *Let us make man*.'"[1] God's grand finale.

When I stand over the Grand Canyon, or a snowy mountain, or listen to waves crash onto the beach, I can get this confused. The rest of creation is so stunning, it often reduces me to tears. God's creativity is so enormous, I can scarcely take it in. Yet as valuable as nature is to Him, what has He declared as His crowning glory? You and me.

Read Psalm 8:3-6. Do you struggle with the question David asks here? If so, why? If not, why do you suppose it was an issue for David?

Everything else was made uniquely. There was no resemblance to anything. It was all a new work. Yet only God's own image was appropriate to bestow on mankind. He took of what was already perfected and grafted it into His finest creation, separating it from everything else. "Let us make man in *our image.*"

This is hard for us. Between oppression from the Enemy and poor teaching from the pulpit, we've boiled down our existence to this: God = good; Man = bad. Yet "God saw all that he had made, and it was very good" (Genesis 1:31). He took of His own excellence and formed mankind in the same likeness, but we are so focused on our deficiencies that we forget to celebrate all that is godly about our humanity.

List several of God's characteristics that you see stamped into the human race.

*Open your ears. What has God communicated to you through people, made in *His* image?

Certainly we've distorted this. Sin didn't take long to discover, and we have an Enemy who prowls. But for a moment, set aside the dark images of this world, and instead focus on the immense goodness. I can't even get beyond my own city limits without astounding examples of generosity, mercy, compassion, love. I've seen people sacrifice, give, encourage, intercede. Friends sit with friends in waiting rooms. Girlfriends clasp hands and pray together. Time is offered. Love is given. Resources are shared. Personalities are celebrated.

Do you think we made up those qualities? Did we just dig deep and find some spare goodness? Our capacity for decency is astonishing. That's why we see nonbelievers constantly demonstrate compassion: Whether or not they acknowledge God, they were created in His image. The way people respond to others in crisis is proof. He wired us with that instinct for compassion. When you look around and see the very best humans have to offer, you are looking in the mirror of heaven. That is God's image we bear. It is no wonder He called us His workmanship. Made in His likeness and imitating His character, mankind emulates the Creator of the universe. Paul called it a dim reflection (see 1 Corinthians 13:12), but it's a reflection nonetheless.

The best of humanity represents the tip of God's goodness.

What does the finest of the human race tell you about God? What is He like?

He constantly talks to me through what I see in people. When I see pictures of devastation around the world and I weep with compassion, God reminds me how Jesus wept over Jerusalem. He created the emotion. When my friends celebrate my victories like they were their own, God whispers, "I fashioned this kind of love between believers. It first existed between My Son and Me." When Brandon and I didn't have two dimes to rub together and groceries appeared on our doorstep, I saw God's generosity exhibited as He prompted His obedient ones to care for us.

I look at the goodness of mankind and say: "You are the kindest, dearest, smartest, most generous, patient, creative, hilarious, loving, fascinating God." If this is how He fashioned us to behave, then my stars!

How much kinder is He?

Of course, this message gets muffled through fallen man.

God is often viewed through the human lens of heartache, because what He made perfect, we distorted. As a loving Creator, He gave us the choice to either display His image or conform to the world that rejected Him. The carnage on that dark path screams so loudly, we misunderstand it to be universal. God's image seems too far gone to recover. And it once was. But Jesus came to right the wrong.

Paul urged us "to put on the new self, *created to be like God* in true righteousness and holiness" (Ephesians 4:24). This new self comes through salvation. There is no other way. God's image has been too corrupted without the renewal of Christ. Yet through Jesus, we bear the stamps of righteousness and holiness, like the imprint of a king on a coin. Can you believe that?

Can you believe that? How does your self-image honor or dishonor God? Remember, you are His handiwork.

According to Scripture, because we are made in God's image:

- Every human being is worthy of honor and respect; he shouldn't be murdered (see Genesis 9:6) nor cursed (see James 3:9).
- We have God-given authority to exercise; we aren't to be His ambivalent puppets (see Genesis 1:26).
- We have an amazing capacity for spiritual knowledge (see Colossians 3:10).
- Eternity is set within our hearts, as it is in God's (see Ecclesiastes 3:11).
- We are individually called, justified, and glorified as we are conformed to the likeness of God's own Son (see Romans 8:29-30).

*Through mankind—the image of God—what is He communicating to you about *you?*

Believer, God loves you so dearly. You are amazing to Him. You bear the image of His beloved Son, His own character even. He has crowned you with glory and honor. Jesus' sacrifice has given you a part in the very holiness of heaven while you walk this earth.

Are you funny? God is hilarious. Are you merciful? He grafted that into your heart straight from His. Those talents? God's. Those amazing gifts? His likeness. All those characteristics that make you unique were born out of His image. You are truly the display of His splendor. It is as clear as if He wrote it on the wall.

Learn to listen to God's voice through the people He created. Listen to what those people communicate about Him. As we were made in His image, know that God has ears to hear your cries. His eyes see every abuse you endure; vengeance is His. Our Father has arms that can comfort like no one else, and His reach is never too short to save. His hands hold you so tightly the Enemy can never snatch you out. You are a fragrant offering to God, a pleasing aroma to His senses. Your enemy will be crushed under God's feet. They never slip. And know this: His mouth constantly speaks to His people.

After all, you are His workmanship.

Have you ever allowed God to speak through His image in mankind? He has much to say. Ask Him to show you His character. If you need to, release the poor idea you've carried of yourself. Ask the Spirit to lead you as the display of God's splendor.

Friendship

You know, God's a Big Guy. He could have done things however He wanted to. Creation was simply a function of His imagination. Knowing that He is excellent, entirely all-knowing, we can be certain this world was formed just right. He didn't shelve any better ideas. God's design was exact.

He could have arranged human relationships any number of ways. We could have been one cohesive group system. He could have made us genderless. Reproduction could have been asexual like amoebas that bud and split (as if we don't basically do that now). Or humanity could have been entirely individualistic. Each to his own. Who knows?

Yet, with perfection at His fingertips, God chose three specific relationships humanity would function within best: friendship, marriage, and parenthood. He took His best ideas and designed the whole world around them. Doesn't it seem God would communicate explicitly through them? This week represents some of my favorite ways He speaks. Today let's look at what God has to say through friendship.

Read Luke 1:5-25. Jot down a summary of Elizabeth from this passage. Who was she? What was she like?

I envision Elizabeth as the ultimate older mentor. She grew up in a priestly family, then married a priest (a really good one). I never judge Zechariah for that doubt of his; there's no question that if an angel ever appeared to me, I'd quickly be struck mute on account of my big mouth. This godly couple, upright and blameless, was given a pregnancy long after they'd lost all hope of one. It's indicative of their goodness that Zechariah was still a priest and Elizabeth was highly regarded, as barrenness was considered divine disfavor then. Their integrity won out over social reproach, and they were ultimately chosen to parent our dearest John the Baptist.

Do you know a woman whose godliness surpasses her painful circumstances? What is she like?

*Read Luke 1:26-38. Why do you think Zechariah's objection (see verse 18) was met with discipline, yet Mary's objection was met with encouragement?

Keep Mary in focus: She was very young, probably early teens, poor, engaged to a carpenter. *A virgin.* That posed a question or two. Other than being in the lineage of David, there was nothing noteworthy about her. She didn't have wealth to soften the hard edges of her new reality. She didn't come from a prestigious family who could spin this or brush it under the carpet. She lived in Nazareth, home of no one important. She wasn't even old enough to have proven her worth as a woman. She was just a young, unmarried, pregnant virgin.

Why do you think Gabriel referred to Elizabeth (see verse 36) as he encouraged Mary? Why not King David or Moses or someone else used for great things?

Mary immediately journeyed from Nazareth down to Judea to sit under Elizabeth's influence. If ever a woman was more in need of a friend, I've never seen it. Against practicality, Mary traveled three days alone not to birth Jesus in secret, not to hide until it was all over, but to be strengthened in God by another woman who loved Him.

*Read Luke 1:39-45. How was Mary probably feeling when she knocked on Elizabeth's door? What do you think Elizabeth's first words to Mary did for her spirit?

Friendship. God is so good. No male voice injected itself on this scene. The house was silent of men. Joseph was in Nazareth. Zechariah had been struck mute, although I wish he and Mary could have talked a bit. ("Hey, what did you think of Gabriel? He scared the bejeebers out of me!" "Me too! I totally freaked out!") There was only Mary and Elizabeth, each miraculously pregnant, one carrying the forerunner of the other.

Don't you know Mary was encouraged for those three months? Didn't Elizabeth love having Mary in her house? As Elizabeth neared the end of her pregnancy, a challenge at her age, and Mary began to grow, struggling through those hard early months, God upheld them both through each other. To build up the mother of Jesus, God didn't choose her fiancé. He didn't choose her parents. He didn't choose a rabbi.

He chose a Girlfriend.

Is there anything better than Girlfriends? Our parents and husbands and children are amazing as we'll get to later, but with our friends we've experienced wifehood and pregnancies and life as women. We wholly understand each other. Where my husband can only say, "I don't understand why you're crying. Did I do this?" my Girlfriends hand me a tissue and completely get me. I've dried their irrational tears, too. While Scripture calls marriage a mystery, it says a friend sticks closer than a brother (see Proverbs 18:24).

List several qualities of a best friend.

Believer, if you've ever received love from a friend, been upheld by one, or laughed together until your side ached, let me introduce you to God: the Ultimate Friend. For humanity, He chose friendship. Why? He gave us this beautiful relationship not just to make life great, but to tell us about Himself. He is the original model. Friendship is set within our hearts to teach us the depth of God's affection.

He called Himself friend of Abraham, friend of Moses. Jesus was a friend of sinners, friend of the lowly. Jesus said to His closest followers, "I no longer call you servants, because a servant does not know his master's business. Instead, I have called you friends" (John 15:15). Indeed, Jesus laid His life down not for His inferiors, but for His friends (see 15:13). This side-by-sideness, this bond of togetherness, is how He feels about you and me. He created us for it.

We often miss this, don't we? With good intentions to keep God high on His throne where He belongs, we overlook His affection for us. Or our faith isn't mature enough to understand that He can be both Almighty and Friend. As Dallas Willard noted,

We demean God immeasurably by casting him in the role of the cosmic boss, foreman or autocrat, whose chief joy in relation to humans is ordering them around, taking pleasure in seeing them jump at his command and painstakingly noting down any failures. Instead we are to be God's friends and fellow workers. The role of taskmaster, whether a pleased one or an angry one, is a role that God accepts only when appointed to it by our own limited understanding.[2]

*Take a look at the friendship qualities you listed earlier. Which of these, if any, do you have a hard time equating with God? Why?

Does your answer shed any light on God's voice to you? How has a poor concept of God as your friend muffled His words? Have you only been listening for orders or rebukes?

God instituted friendship to demonstrate His character. He chose a relationship we could get our arms around. While many of His ways are beyond us, in the model of friendship, we get it. Friends make sense to us. We understand that a friend laughs with us, sometimes at us. We know a friend wants to spend time together just for the good company. We can comprehend a friend who sits at a bedside by us or carries our burdens. Our best friend can speak truth, even when it's painful. We know she loves us still. We understand that a friend holds our hand and says, "Let's do this together."

That's God.

*What does God want to communicate to you as the Ultimate Friend? What is He saying?

This friendship model helps us understand His voice better. It allows us to weed out the Enemy's voice quicker. As our friend, God pursues our company. He presses in despite our attempts to ignore Him. He carries the load for us when it becomes overwhelming. When I'm trying to understand Him, I often ask: What would a friend do? Love me? Encourage me? Enjoy me? Push me to my potential? Point me to the Word? Because that's what God does. I know Him as that friend.

What wouldn't a friend do? He wouldn't shame me. He wouldn't diminish my gifts or reconstitute my insecurities. He'll never support my jealousies. He won't justify my poor choices. He'd never turn His back on me or hold grudges after I've apologized. That's the voice of the Enemy. Don't listen to any of that.

Read Luke 1:46-56. How does this Mary differ from the one we read in verses 34-38?

For three months, Elizabeth blessed Mary. She spoke truth and reinforced Mary's faith when anyone else would have judged her. Though her culture esteemed the elder over the younger, Elizabeth greatly respected teenage Mary. She provided a safe place for Mary when she needed it most. Through friendship, Mary was transformed from a hesitantly obedient girl to a confident psalmist speaking magnificent praises well beyond her youth.

That is the magic of a godly friend.

Believer, the next time you encounter the magic, turn a grateful eye toward heaven and thank the Friend who invented the concept. He created friendship to bless you, but ultimately to characterize your relationship with Him. He speaks to you as a Best Friend. *That's* the voice you need to listen for.

As God intended all along, our friends with flesh and bones show us the way. Karla Worley said it well in her book *Traveling Together*: "Our friendship is a model of the kingdom, a living demonstration. The Word becomes flesh. Our friendship is the chalkboard upon which God explains Himself. . . . That is the purpose for which He draws us to His side and to each other."[3]

Girls, do you talk to God as your Friend? Do you hear Him as a Friend? This was His design from the beginning. Ask the Spirit to help you lay aside any misconceptions about your relationship. Pray to know God like this.

Marriage

My Girlfriend Jen is possibly the funniest person I've ever known. She has what some call a teeny-weeny shopping problem. With online banking, her husband, Erik says he can track Jen in real time by her debits.

Jen has a penchant for makeup and hair products. In Austin, the mothership of beauty supply stores is called Ulta. As Jen once bought a sixty-dollar pair of tweezers there, you can imagine the possible marital damage it represents. However, Jen realized that she possessed a Get-Out-of-Jail-Free card when, after Erik reviewed her numerous debits, he discovered an eighty-dollar expense at Ulta and said, "Jen! How could you have spent eighty dollars at a gas station? Did you get a car wash or something?" Realizing that Erik had mistaken her favorite salon for a QuikTrip, she said what any of us would have:

"I guess I did."

Now she restricts Ulta purchases to a fifty-dollar limit—a gas tank worth of eyeliner and leave-in conditioner. Marital bliss is temporarily intact. At least until Erik drives by Ulta and sees not one solitary gas pump.

Ah, marriage. Such an adventure. Two adults voluntarily joined together, accepting each other, warts and all, combining opposite personalities, and making a go of it. Between the basic flaws of two people, it's a miracle any marriage works out. Yet with a firm commitment, a couple can go to the grave still in love—even if one partner gets her gas at a beauty store.

God chose marriage for humanity. Why? To crack Himself up? I'm sure that happens, but the Word tells us a more accurate story. Not only was marriage instituted to bless us (yes it was), but it demonstrates a relationship we have with God that transcends obligation. It is birthed out of choice: His and ours.

Let's go back to the upcoming marriage of Mary and Joseph and see what we can learn about God. But first, there is something important to understand about the Jews. Unlike today, when an engagement is often nothing more than a trial period, in Mary and Joseph's day, being engaged was the same as being married. Literally. In the case of infidelity, a man could not renounce his fiancée except by divorce. If a man died while he was engaged, his fiancée was legally declared a widow. And, most important to our story, if she was unfaithful, she could be punished for adultery under the laws of marriage.

Not only that, but according to Jewish tradition, Joseph and Mary would have already gone through an espousal, a formal proceeding following the selection of the bride, confirmed by oaths, and sealed with presents to the bride's family. The whole affair was already celebrated with a feast involving both families.[4] Past the point of no return was an understatement.

Given all that, read Matthew 1:18. What do you think raced through Joseph's mind?

Infidelity is the blackest betrayal. A friend of mine said the carnage is almost indescribable, as her emotional devastation translated to physical. She explained how her stomach lurched and she sat in the bathroom rocking and waiting to throw up. She felt like she had been repeatedly kicked in the stomach. On some level, life would never again be the same. This is a familiar reality to some of you, too.

Let's make a transition to the model of marriage God created. The relationships are specific: Jesus called Himself the bridegroom, the church His bride. Some teachers present this relationship in a way that makes me feel, well, weirded out. They highlight the romantic aspects of a human marriage ("Jesus has picked out your favorite music. He's spinning you around the dance floor," and so on). That's fine. But Jesus is not David Koresh with a harem. The bride of Christ is not you specifically. It's all of us collectively: His church. His people.

This relationship is born out of choice just like any marriage. God first loved us. He didn't have to. He wanted to. "For he chose us in him before the creation of the world to be holy and blameless in his sight" (Ephesians 1:4). He picked mankind to unite with. Why? He loves us. Pure and simple. He really does.

*What characteristics of a bridegroom do you see in Jesus as He relates to you?

*What do you think He's expecting from His church as the bride?

Mary and Joseph both understood what married people should expect from each other. God chose them well. Notice how Joseph reacted *before* the angel clued him in.

Read Matthew 1:19-25. The law allowed for Mary to be stoned for adultery. What does verse 19 tell you about Joseph?

Believer, Jesus knew betrayal, too. He was rejected by the

people He came to love. He hung, ridiculed, while they cried, "Crucify Him!" He was spit on, mocked, beaten, laughed at. Yet our Bridegroom begged from the cross: "Father, forgive them, for they do not know what they are doing" (Luke 23:34). He had the power to escape the cross in retaliation. He could have abandoned His mission and left us all to death. Yet, like Joseph, He chose forgiveness. Mercy. Grace. He is the Bridegroom who loves His bride, even when she betrays Him.

As God explained to Hosea, whose adulterous marriage represented God's relationship with His people: "Go, show your love to your wife again, though she is loved by another and is an adulteress. Love her as the LORD loves the Israelites, though they turn to other gods" (Hosea 3:1). God chose marriage, because through its example, we begin to understand His forgiveness, His faithfulness. We learn to listen to Him through this grid. That's why God used comparisons in the Word that we can relate to.

What is God communicating to you through the following Scriptures:

I delight greatly in the LORD;
   my soul rejoices in my God.
For he has clothed me with garments of salvation
   and arrayed me in a robe of righteousness,
as a bridegroom adorns his head like a priest,
   and as a bride adorns herself with her jewels.
     (Isaiah 61:10)

As a bridegroom rejoices over his bride,
   so will your God rejoice over you. (Isaiah 62:5)

Husbands, love your wives, just as Christ loved the church and gave himself up for her to make her holy, cleansing her by the washing with water through the word, and to present her to himself as a radiant church, without stain or wrinkle or any other blemish, but holy and blameless. (Ephesians 5:25-27)

How do you think God speaks to His bride? What is His tone? Why?

God first presented marriage in pure form, with clear boundaries and beautiful roles for each partner to fill. It was meant as a blessing, a union of joy. The original design was intended to be a reflection of His relationship with us. Obviously, humanity hasn't done a great job with marriage. But don't allow the flaws of mankind to ruin this parallel in your spiritual marriage. Don't ever expect God's voice to sound critical or controlling. Neither should you expect Him to throw His hands up at every mistake you make and wish He'd chosen someone else.

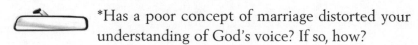 *Has a poor concept of marriage distorted your understanding of God's voice? If so, how?

Think of the godliest, healthiest marriage you know. Through its example, what does it tell you about God? About the relationship He wants with you?

God is altogether faithful. He will never betray you. He won't leave you for someone better. Your relationship is no accident. He chose you. God jealously hovers over you in protection—you are His ultimate concern. You're safe. As the provider in this union, the Lord owns the cattle on a thousand hills. He can take care of you. Don't worry. And though you may periodically reject Him, there is always forgiveness. Every time. God's final goal is to usher you into heaven clean, blameless. He works tirelessly to that end every single day of your life.

To Him, you're worth it.

This is a union to celebrate.

Then I heard what sounded like a great multitude, like the roar of rushing waters and like loud peals of thunder, shouting: "Hallelujah! For our Lord God Almighty reigns. Let us rejoice and be glad and give him glory! For the wedding of the Lamb has come, and his bride has made herself ready." (Revelation 19:6-7)

What does God want to communicate to you through the model of marriage? What aspect of your relationship have you misunderstood? Ask the Spirit to open your ears today. With His help, search the depths of communication within this covenant relationship He chose you for.

Parenthood

My second-grader, Gavin, is the sweetest soul wrapped in a tiny package. He's a head shorter and twenty pounds lighter than his peers, though he has no idea. When he was in first grade, I got a call one morning from the school nurse that Gavin had been punched in the eye by a bigger kid in the cafeteria for sitting where the aide told him to (which apparently was saved for this degenerate's friend). He was hurt and embarrassed and sitting in her office with an ice pack.

Now, I'm normally a peace-loving girl. I'm kind to animals. I don't curse at bad drivers, though I want to. I'm a general fan of goodwill. But that morning, my nice little heart started to throb and turn a dark shade of black.

First, I had to get to my baby and make it all better. I had to hold him and let the tears flow that I knew he was holding back. Second, I wanted to find that punk kid and grind him down to mere crumbs as a service to society, because he was destined to a life of drugs and petty theft, no doubt. *Who punches a first grader the size of a three-year-old?*

My friends—all parents—got in on the rage:

"Do you want me to take out a hit on him?"

"Should I wait for him after school and run him down with my car?"

"I know a guy. I'm just saying people can disappear."

I feel comfortable ratting out my ugliness in print because I know, without a doubt, all the moms out there are saying, "Sing it, Sister." You'd have felt the same way. Our kids evoke something in us that goes beyond description. For their sake, there is nothing we won't do. We'll take down the administration of an entire school system, so help us. We'll move. We'll sacrifice. We'll advocate relentlessly. We will leave thirty-four messages until the right person calls us back.

William Makepeace Thackeray said, "Mother is the name for God in the lips and hearts of little children."[5] Believer, God gave us parenthood, knowing full well it would be our life's greatest work, the passion of our existence—just as we are of His. If any one earthly relationship established by God teaches me most about how to hear Him, it's this one. No matter how much I don't understand, how badly I screw up, or how scared I get, I always return to the same truth:

I am God's daughter.

More than any other relational term, God called Himself "Father." Overcome with the ramifications of this bond, John declared: "How great is the love the Father has lavished on us, that we should be called children of God!" (1 John 3:1). Understanding this dynamic is critical to effectively hearing God's voice.

Let's look back at Mary and Joseph and see what God has to show us through parenthood. Of course, the birth of Jesus was not what Mary dreamed of as she looked forward to motherhood. Pregnant out of wedlock (but innocent, as hardly anyone believed), Mary was forced to walk seventy miles to Bethlehem at her due date. Can we say uncomfortable? There was no midwife to assist her during her delivery. No one even offered a decent bed to labor on. She delivered Jesus alone in a cold barn, possibly a cave. While Elizabeth's delivery of John was met with joy by friends and neighbors, Mary gave birth in utter isolation and humility. She was probably thirteen or so.

Read Luke 2:4-19. Though we'd expect to find her despairing, how did God encourage Mary?

Matthew Henry said of these wonders: "The virgin Mary made them the matter of her private meditation. She said little, but kept all these things, and pondered them in her heart . . . it is satisfaction enough to find that, if no one else takes notice of the birth of her child, angels do."[6]

I can understand her treasures. Even without the sweet shepherds and angels speaking the praises of her baby, she knew the miracle of parenthood. If you're a mother, remember the first time you looked at your baby? The pain that brought you to that moment is forgotten. The emotions are astonishing. The love is instantaneous. Flesh of your flesh. It almost cannot be described. I could cry right now just thinking about it.

As a parent, how do you think God feels about a new believer the moment she is ushered into His family by faith?

Mary gives us another fine example of God's love for us as His children. Read Luke 2:41-52. How do you think Mary would have described those three days?

Verse 51 tells us that "his mother treasured all these things in her heart." Now, I lost a kid in Dillards for twenty minutes, and I nearly had a coronary. The adrenaline alone nearly sent me into a coma. He wasn't conferring with rabbis; he was hiding in one of the rounds. The only thing I treasured that day was getting out of there without having filed a missing-child report. I don't think I went back to the mall for six months.

But Mary took the good, the scary, the confusing, the proud moments, the memories—all of it—and treasured it. Even on the heels of discipline. That's parenting. We don't get to pick and choose which experiences we'd like to have. Our kids have strong wills. Sometimes they make choices we want to broadcast. Other times they send us to the medicine cabinet. They make us cry and laugh and work and swoon. And we love them through it all. They are our kids. We cannot distance ourselves from partiality.

*Since we're made in His image, what does this tell you about God as a parent?

We often think we can fall out of favor with God. Our relationship seems conditional. He is so good and right, all of our wrongs just seem like deal breakers. Or, on a lesser scale, we simply don't understand His love for us. His pride in us. His patience for us. His forgiveness of us. Believer, God can no more separate Himself from His adoration of you than you can of your own children.

This is how He speaks to you.

He wants to tell you how much He loves you. God wants to build you up and steer you away from danger. He really wants to teach you. The Word and Spirit stand ready. God plans on raising you to maturity, so He'll discipline you to that end. He has never once expected you to be perfect. But you are still His treasure.

Do you have a misconception about God's voice that is contradictory to His role as your Father? If so, what have you misconstrued? Have you thought of Him as scary? Cold? A taskmaster?

*Think of your most challenging circumstance right now. As your parent, what do you think God wants to tell you? What would you say if it were your child?

Maybe the finest demonstration of godly parenthood came through Joseph. He had every reason to feel disconnected from Jesus. After all, he wasn't Jesus' dad. He fathered at least four other boys and girls who bore his resemblance, unlike Jesus. His birth represented a time when Joseph was ridiculed, possibly pitied. In the opinion of others, Joseph played the fool. Mary had eyes for another; Jesus was living proof of it. For Joseph, it would have been tempting to make a clear distinction between Jesus and his other kids.

Yet he raised Jesus as his own. In the spirit of adoption, Joseph loved Jesus as his son. The Word never once tells us that Joseph threw his hands up and said, "Well, what are you going to do? He's not my son, I'll tell you that right now!" Eight days after His birth, he consecrated Jesus to God as the firstborn male of his household. He journeyed to *Egypt* to protect Him from Herod. He feared for Jesus' life as any father would. Joseph passed his trade on to Jesus, working side-by-side over wood and nails. In fact, when Jesus began blowing people away with His teaching in the local synagogue, the people said in amazement: "Isn't this Joseph's son?" (Luke 4:22).

Girls, you and I have been adopted as believers. Because of the human condition, we weren't born into God's family. But like any earthly adoption, He has given us an opportunity we would never have had otherwise. The prince of this world would keep us as orphans—lonely, poor, abandoned. Yet through Jesus, we've been adopted into the family of the King of Kings. We've become royalty.

As John explained, "To all who received him, to those who believed in his name, he gave the right to become children of God—children born not of natural descent, nor of human decision or a husband's will, but born of God" (John 1:12-13).

 *What do you think a parent wants to especially communicate to his adopted child?

Hear Him, Believer. When you're not sure, ask: Is this what a Father would say to His daughter? Look around at parenthood the way God established it, and discover your heavenly Father.

Do you feel like you keep a constant eye on your kids, desperate for their safety? "The LORD will watch over your coming and going both now and forevermore" (Psalm 121:8).

Do you wish your kids could understand why you discipline them? "The LORD disciplines those he loves, as a father the son he delights in" (Proverbs 3:12).

Ever want to secure vengeance for your child? "Leave room for God's wrath, for it is written: 'It is mine to avenge; I will repay,' says the Lord" (Romans 12:19).

Are you your children's biggest cheerleader? Meet "God our Father, who loved us and by his grace gave us eternal encouragement and good hope" (2 Thessalonians 2:16).

Listen for these conversations. Allow Him to speak to you simply through the model of parenthood. He created it. It emulates the very relationship between Him and His beloved Son. Unbreakable. Impenetrable. Unshakeable. Eternal.

"I will be a Father to you, and you will be my sons and daughters," says the Lord Almighty (2 Corinthians 6:18).

You can't hear God if you don't know what to listen for. He is your Father. Be His daughter today. Ask Him to speak His love and adoration and protection over you. Ask the Spirit to help you hear it.

Tune In

Hosea is a dark, powerful book full of imagery and symbolism. It beautifully characterizes our relationship with God, both as His children and His wandering bride. Although once unified, the Holy Land was divided into two parts (the northern kingdom of Israel and the southern kingdom of Judah) after Solomon's death in 930 BC. Around 750 BC, the prophet Hosea warned the northerners (sometimes called Ephraim after Israel's largest tribe) that Assyria was about to destroy Israel. The people rejected his message and were conquered in 722 BC. That marked the end of Israel, and ten of the twelve original tribes were lost forever until God raises them up again in the last days. Only the tribes of Judah and Benjamin remained in the south.

As a physical manifestation of God's theme—His steadfast love for Israel despite her unfaithfulness—He asked Hosea to take an adulterous wife. Their three children bore symbolic names representing God's message. To display His faithfulness, the Lord instructed Hosea to take his wife back and love her in spite of her betrayals, a living example of forgiveness.

Pray for the Spirit to teach you truth about God today. Ask Him to open your ears to the relationship God wants with you. As you pray and journal through each section, regard the questions simply as a guide. They are not a list to be answered. They are there to show you how to ask healthy questions of Scripture. Use one or several, or let the Spirit lead you otherwise.

Let's read God's words to Israel as He begged them to repent and turn back to Him. Remember: He was trying to spare them from captivity but could do so only if they obeyed Him.

Read Hosea 11:1-2.

- How did God display fatherhood when He first took His son, Israel, out of Egypt? What parental characteristics did He exhibit?
- Why do you think Israel's freedom paved the way for their rebellion? How does that happen with us?
- The more God called, the faster they ran from Him. Do you ever do that? Why?
- What idols take God's place in your life?

Read Hosea 11:3-4.

- See how tender God is! These are *His* words, not a poet's. As a young believer, how did God teach you to walk? How did He hold your arms?
- What do these verses tell you about how God feels about His young believers? How does He care for them?
- How has God led you with cords of human kindness? Who has He tangibly used to love on you?
- Why can't we recognize the hand that feeds us sometimes? Does this have anything to do with the way we listen to Him?

Read Hosea 11:5-7.

- What does captivity look like for us today? What do we have to do in order to be spared?
- God referenced the "end of their plans." How do your plans get in the way of childlike obedience to your heavenly Father?
- Are you determined to turn from God right now? Is He begging you to come back? What keeps you in rebellion?

Read Hosea 11:8-9.

- Admah and Zeboiim were cities overthrown when Sodom was destroyed because of sin. Why did God view Israel (also called Ephraim) differently? They were also in sin.
- How does this characterize a forgiving husband and an adulterous wife? What is God telling you about Himself?
- God made a distinction regarding His compassion: "I am God, and not man." Do you need to hear that, Believer? How are you hung up on this?

Girls, learning to hear God begins and ends with knowing Him. You'll never find a mature believer who doesn't recognize God's voice. It's not an issue for her, because it's as clear as the voice of her best friend, as distinct as her husband's, as plain as her own dad's. Discovering Him through the relationships He created is to deepen your understanding, which in turn makes what He is saying audible.

When you fail to recognize the godliness of your humanity made in His image, you also miss it when He says, "You are My handiwork. I'm so proud." If you've never known Him as a friend who enjoys your company, you're not going to hear Him when He says, "Sit with Me awhile. I like you." It would be beyond your ability to understand that. A woman who doesn't get that God honors a binding covenant with her as a husband to a wife isn't prepared to hear, "I forgive you. Nothing you can do will make me leave you." It will fall on deaf ears. If you don't realize that, as His child, God sometimes speaks to you only to shower you with love, not criticize your faults, you'd miss it when He declared, "You are my crowning work." You probably have a hard time living in grace.

Open your eyes, Believer; open your ears. He has spoken through the image of mankind and the relationships He established for us. And it's a good word. He just might never sound the same to you again.

He Speaks Through His Spirit

(DANIEL)

Spiritual Gifts

There are certain things no one felt the need to tell me about having a baby. Oh sure, there was lots of talk about onesies and Diaper Genies and monitors. The safe stuff. However, no one told me that my boobs would enlarge to the size of two bowling balls and become about the same density. Everyone forgot to mention how I'd still look six months pregnant with a gooey jelly belly post-delivery. You could've lost a hand in there. Who knew I'd be so sore afterward that I swore to my husband I had birthed our son out of my behind? Thanks for nothing, Everyone I Know.

But perhaps nothing took me by shock more than the breast pump. When I opened that box and saw those tubes and bottles and suspicious-looking oil funnels, I went straight to the fetal position. What went where? What were those buttons? Why does it sound like a generator? I didn't even know such a torture device still existed much less have any clue what to do with it. I had a sneaking suspicion those funnels wanted to cannibalize my nipples, but since a gentle breeze across my breasts caused me to scream in agony, I decided to pass on this experiment and use the cones as kitchen tools. That is, until my bowling balls started leaking uncontrollably.

Chalk that up to one more surprise.

There is a specific way God has spoken to every believer. He gave us something to use, and it was very clear to Him. He knew just what He wanted to accomplish with it. What He presented had an obvious purpose that should have been as plain as day. Yet we've confused it. Quite frankly, it scares a lot of us. We have no idea what to do with it. In fact, many of us scratched our heads at it and set it aside or used it for something else. But God couldn't have been clearer when He sent the Holy Spirit to deliver the goods:

Your spiritual gift.

There is hardly a plainer objective He has communicated to me. Sometimes when I'm spazzing out, as I'm prone to do, God grabs me by the shoulders and says, "Let's review. What are you good at? What did I ask you to do with that? Are you doing it? There's your red flag. Go back to what you know." The use of my spiritual gifts has brought me back to center more times that I can count. It has been the tool that helped me unclutter my schedule and gave me the confirmation to say "no." It allows me to check my obedience and take inventory of my purpose.

If you are a believer, you certainly have one or more gifts. Paul explained it like this: "There are different kinds of gifts, but the same Spirit. . . . Now to each one the manifestation of the Spirit is given for the common good" (1 Corinthians 12:4,7). That gift is given at salvation, but it develops as spiritual maturity grows.

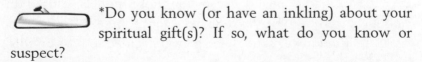 *Do you know (or have an inkling) about your spiritual gift(s)? If so, what do you know or suspect?

We're looking at a man this week whose story gives us so many examples of God's voice, it could've taken up this entire study: Daniel. Before we launch into it, there's a bit to understand about his circumstances. You remember how Hosea prophesied against the northern kingdom of Israel concerning their captivity by Assyria (Day 5 of last week)? Their disregard brought it to pass in 722 BC. Well, a little over one hundred years later, Jeremiah and Isaiah and other prophets were bringing the same message of repentance to the southern kingdom of Judah and its rebellious King Jehoiakim. Turn from idolatry or be captured. Big shock: they didn't listen.

Whereas one hundred years earlier Assyria was the world

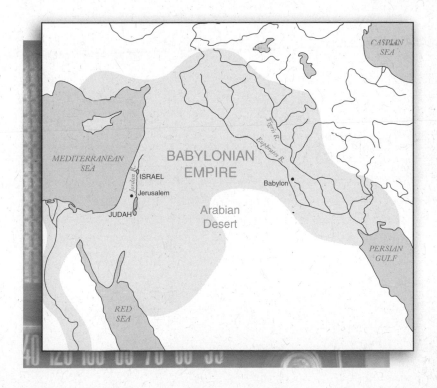

THE BABYLONIAN EMPIRE

power, Babylon now dominated (see map on previous page). And, as the prophets predicted, they had their sights set on Judah. God warned through Jeremiah: "I will hand all Judah over to the king of Babylon, who will carry them away to Babylon or put them to the sword" (Jeremiah 20:4). It wasn't a gray area, but no one cared. No sooner had Nebuchadnezzar taken the Babylonian throne than he invaded Judah and carted off the first wave of captives to Babylon. They included young Daniel and his friends. They were probably in their midteens.

Read Daniel 1:1-7. Though he could have taken anyone from Jerusalem, Nebuchadnezzar gave specific instructions on whom to capture. What was he up to? What do you think his strategy was?

Smart, that one. Neb even took their significant Jewish names and gave them pagan names honoring his gods. The boys must have felt disgusted, even defiled. But you know what? You can take God out of a name, out of school, out of a pledge, out of an entire country, but you can't take Him out of a heart.

We start to see an interesting progression through the example of Daniel. God predisposed him toward his gifts, as verse 4 demonstrates. He had some natural abilities and intelligence. God gave him the bare bones of his gifts as a young believer, the raw material. They still needed to develop, but the arrows began pointing in a certain direction.

*Can you see this similarity in your life? If you know your gifts, can you recall the early indicators of them?

If you're not sure, what does it seem God has predisposed you toward? Teaching? Showing mercy? Leadership? Check out the list of spiritual gifts in Romans 12:6-8 and see if you don't recognize your own reflection. (That's not an exhaustive list, so don't worry if none of it sounds like you.)

I used to line up my dolls and teach them relentlessly when my sisters wouldn't indulge me. Plus, I had a crazy passion for the Bible from a really young age. As in: Nerd Alert. At eighteen, my life's calling wasn't clear to me yet, but I knew enough to major in education. I married a pastor. The focus began narrowing. In my twenties, my love for teaching bred with my love for the Lord and became ignited by my love for women, and here I sit today typing away for you. For God. It was fuzzy ten years ago, but looking back now, I see God's hand was preparing me.

Our engagement with our gifts is a component that we can't ignore. As God begins leading us in a certain direction, we must go along willingly. It's our responsibility to show ourselves obedient. This is usually a series of baby steps, but you string enough of those together, and you've traveled miles down the road of spiritual growth, paving the way for the development of your gifts. That's what Daniel did, too.

Read Daniel 1:8-16. What traits did Daniel exhibit here? List everything you see in him.

As Jews committed to God, Daniel and the boys were well aware that the meat on Nebuchadnezzar's table was (1) ceremonially unclean according to Jewish law, neither slaughtered nor prepared as God had commanded, and (2) offered to idols when slaughtered. A portion of the king's wine had also been poured out on a pagan altar before landing on their table. God had already spoken clearly on this matter: "No way." It wasn't conditional on Daniel's location or circumstance. It was a nonnegotiable of holiness, and Daniel was resolved to obey it.

Is there anything God has spoken clearly to you about, but you find yourself shirking obedience? Have you allowed circumstances to justify your disobedience? How so?

Certainly Daniel was taking a large risk. He could have easily fallen out of favor for disobeying the king. After all, he was a Jewish captive in a foreign country. He didn't exactly rank high on the "I'll do what I want" list. He'd been taken by force, no doubt a witness to the massacre of many of his people along the way. He was at the mercy of a ruthless leader who'd just as soon dispose of him than deal with the insurgency of a teenager.

Yet Daniel used the diplomatic skills God had given him to reason, negotiate, and ultimately secure safe obedience to his King of Kings. What a kid! He passed the test with flying colors. It seems this demonstration of obedience moved God to dump the whole package on Daniel and the boys.

Read Daniel 1:17-21. Why do you think God chose these gifts for Daniel and his friends? Any thoughts?

Believer, God is so a God of the Big Plan. Nothing is random. He gifts His people to accomplish His specific work. The work has many layers, so we have many different gifts. He designed His kingdom to be a well-oiled machine carried forward by intentional obedience through the execution of our talents. Yet He looks down on many of us holding our little gift in our hands asking, "What am I supposed to do with this?"

Simply through the gift itself, God has spoken clearly to you. Not only has He revealed His vision for you, but He has also communicated what He sees as your greatest potential. Do you have the gift of mercy? Wow. God must think so highly of the depths of your compassion. Are you an administrator? God loves His organizers. You have special communion with Him. Talk about made in His image! What a word God is giving you! He has taken you into full account, calculated your perfect niche through the Spirit, and carved out your place in this world. This is an earful.

 *What is God saying to you through your spiritual gifts? What does He think of you?

*Take it further. What is He telling you to do with them? Don't know? Ask.

God speaks in many ways. Some formats are heard louder than others. Some are reserved only for certain people. But God communicates through spiritual gifts to every single believer. It is that important. He has something big to say. Through this particular word, He has equipped His children to love, to serve, to minister. We become His very hands and feet, touching this world and delivering the best news it has ever heard. Listen up. You don't want to miss this.

Believer, do you need to discover your gift(s)? God wants you to know it. Spend time with the Spirit today asking Him to point you in the right direction. Do you need to use your gift(s)? Ask Him to show you where. Are you already celebrating your gift(s)? Thank Him. There is nothing better in this world.

Dreams and Visions

I am such a dreamer. Literally. My mind conjures up such strange images during the night, it would seem I am either stoned or a little insane. I'm hoping it's no indicator of my stability, but why else would I dream that my college humanities professor made an announcement in class that I was pregnant and I protested that I was a virgin and everyone started calling me "Mary," upon which I loaded up my neighbor's minivan and drove to Dallas where I was supposed to cheer for my high school basketball team but I couldn't fit into my uniform so I had to leave the back unzipped? Was that because of the baby? I don't know. I was a virgin in my dream, so maybe I was just fat.

But do you see what I'm saying? I'm probably crazy, and dreaming is my only outlet. However, as we continue to seek out God's voice, we're going to turn an eye to dreams and visions today. It's obviously not my listening format, but it does happen, so let's dig in.

First, let's make a simple biblical distinction between dreams and visions. While we could explore it further, basically a dream occurs during sleep, and a vision occurs while awake. Sometimes the line is blurry. But in either case, the recipient is consciously detached from his actual surroundings. This detachment separates dreams and visions from all other forms of godly communication. So for our purposes, we'll study them jointly.

In *Hearing God's Voice*, Henry Blackaby further explains the dreams and visions God sent to biblical people: "First, they were never sought by the recipients but came at God's initiative at unexpected moments. Second, the dreams were not about minor affairs but usually involved matters of great significance."[1]

Dreams and visions played a large role with Daniel, too. Interestingly, many of his experiences did not involve his own dreams but those of a pagan king. As we read yesterday, one of Daniel's gifts was interpreting dreams. If that seems a little kooky to you, remember he was a prophet. If he could see the future with God's help, what's a little dream?

Read Daniel 2:1-9. God (according to 2:28) gave a prophetic dream to a godless king who had captured God's own people. What do you make of this? What does this tell you about how God communicates?

Listen, I tried hard while I was researching to boil dreams and visions down to a formula. I really wanted to say, "Well, dreams basically came to these kinds of people in these kinds of circumstances. See there? That's how God works." But instead, I found that God spoke through dreams to His favorites, His enemies, the spiritually mature, the spiritually simple, prophetically, circumstantially, with the help of angels, with just His voice, through images (some literal, some symbolic), as a terrifying word, and as a wonderful word.

See there? That's how God works.

He will communicate to whomever He wants, however He wants. Our merits or deficiencies, even our salvation or lack thereof, can't hinder or activate God's voice in terms of dreams and visions. They are His doing as He sees fit. Period. What we can learn from Scripture is that God always had a specific agenda when He used this method of speaking. It wasn't a regular form of communication for anyone's day-to-day life. God spoke through dreams somewhat more often when His people lived in pagan cultures (such as Egypt or Babylon) that put a lot of stock in dreams.

In Daniel's life, God gave prophetic dreams to a pagan king that no other "enchanter, magician, or diviner" in the land could make sense of. Granted, Nebuchadnezzar expected them to interpret a dream he had forgotten, but he had some issues. God was stirring this pot for divine reasons.

Read the following passages from Daniel and jot down what you think God's objective was.

2:10-11

2:12-16

2:17-18

2:19-23

2:26-28; 46-47

2:48-49

Nice! All this through a dream and its interpretation. God knew just what He was doing. Daniel's good preaching, or even his advanced intelligence, could never have accomplished this. No, God understood just how to get His work done, though He was dealing with a mule-headed Babylonian king and a Jewish captive. Through one dream, God extracted praises from an enemy's mouth and advanced His servant over every wise man in the province of Babylon.

You can see how dreams and their interpretations became coveted. Were it not for Daniel, every astrologer in the land would have been "cut into pieces and their houses turned into rubble" for not rightly decoding Nebuchadnezzar's dream. Unfortunately, back in Jerusalem, dreams and visions quickly transcended God's purposes and were bartered for power. A host of false prophets rose up among God's people during this time, citing their dreams as "God's word." They led His people astray. It became a huge problem. So by the time Daniel was in his midthirties, God let Babylon wipe Judah and Jerusalem off the map.

Here we learn another principle as we seek God's voice today. On the one hand, do I think He still speaks through dreams and visions? Without a doubt. I know too many godly people who've been led quite clearly through a dream.

*Have you ever had a dream or vision from God? If so, what did He tell you? If not, how do you respond to the idea of dreams and visions at this point?

On the other hand, where we need to be careful is this: It's not appropriate to expect or ask God to speak regularly to us through dreams. The only consistency in Scripture is that God initiated this communication as an exception, not a rule. In fact, dreams were biblically presented as inferior to God's other forms of speaking.

Jeremiah was a prophet in Jerusalem before and during the Babylonian captivity. He was several decades older than Daniel, and he had a lot to say about the problem of too many self-proclaimed visionaries.

Read Jeremiah 23:25-29. How did God describe these dreams? Why?

This is powerful teaching. Dreams are straw, but the Word

of God is grain—nourishing, substantial, filling. The Lord can surely use straw when He needs to. Land sakes, He has spoken through the mouth of a donkey to get His point across. But His clear word delivered to your *active mind* is a fire that refines you, a hammer that breaks you for His purposes.

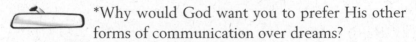 *Why would God want you to prefer His other forms of communication over dreams?

Not that God won't use this method of speaking, because I'm convinced He still does. In those cases, the dreams won't contradict Scripture or God's character. They can be confirmed with prayer and godly counsel and, ultimately, your own peace of mind. God wants you to know what He's saying. As He explained of His communication to His simple servant, Moses: "[I speak] clearly and not in riddles" (Numbers 12:8).

But how much better is it to come before the throne, with all our faculties in place, seeking to know the God of the heavens and hear His plain words? It's the difference between listening to a French language tape during your sleep and standing at the top of the Eiffel Tower eating a croissant with Pierre. Straw versus grain, my friends.

What is your history with God and dreams? Review it with Him. Ask for clarity today and forever to rightly understand His voice, whether it comes during the day or during the night.

Conviction and Obedience

I recently decided to do a morning out with my kids, who were on school break. And by "decided to do a morning out," I mean I had to get out of the house before one of the children got sacrificed to the noise gods to appease them and bring me tranquility. I gave a few last-minute directions before we could leave: "Turn off the TV upstairs, put away your game, and get your water bottles."

Does that seem confusing to you? I didn't think it did either, but although I repeated that phrase seven times, not one kid obeyed. They kept running around, annoying each other, and completely ignoring me. In a moment of parenting resolve, I determined not to go crazy. Not to start hollering like a chimpanzee. Not to flick one of them on the head. I just sat down and waited.

After another five minutes, they finally remembered I was there and stood in front of me: "Why aren't we going? Why are you just sitting there?" *I am calm. I am soft-spoken. I am Mother Teresa.* "Oh? Have our plans intersected again?" I asked. Blank stares. Sarcasm is lost on kindergartners. Finally, I got to say it: "I was just waiting for one person to do what I asked."

Believer, if any one thing moves God to speak, it is our obedience. Sometimes we're so busy running around doing our own thing that we've forgotten God is sitting there. No doubt He has told us things to do, but gracious! We're busy! Yet His history declares that those who do His will can hear His voice. Always. Each time. Every one of them.

Again through a dream, Daniel interpreted that Babylon would soon bend to the powers of the Medes and Persians. World domination was a wandering mistress back then. Sure enough, Cyrus—the young emperor of the Medes and Persians—attacked Babylon. He put the province in charge of an older Mede named Darius (see Daniel 5:30-31).

Read Daniel 6:1-3. At this point, Daniel had been in leadership in Babylon for sixty-seven years, but this new king, Darius, had no history with him. New management was up for grabs, yet Darius still chose Daniel. How do you imagine this set with all those *Babylonian* satraps under the charge of this Jew?

In fact, read Daniel 6:4-9. Has anyone ever turned your godliness against you—maybe at school, or even in a workplace setting—like this? If so, what was it like?

What a testimony. Girls, if someone wanted to scrutinize every aspect of my life, I guarantee they'd find plenty. "King, we report that she is unworthy because she suffers from road rage. She also tells her youngest son that he only has to nap for one minute, then lies and says that's how long it was after he wakes up. In addition, she's very mouthy and frequently blurts out inappropriate opinions. Plus, she's neither shrewd nor diligent, as she pays for a gym membership that she hasn't used in five months."

You know those guys looked hard. They really tried, but

they couldn't find one thing to bring against Daniel. Not even a little matter they could exaggerate. He was entirely trustworthy, neither corrupt nor negligent. That is a life lived unto God: excellence in all things for an excellent Lord. Though he found himself captive in a foreign country, cut off from his family and religion, Daniel chose integrity. He never *once* allowed his circumstances to spoil his loyalty to God or the use of his gifts.

*Read Daniel 6:10-11. Knowing yourself, if you were Daniel, would you have taken a month off and just prayed in your heart? Or would you have kept up the whole routine, kneeling and everything? Why?

Obedience. God requires it. But He also honors it. Interestingly, the satraps wrote the injunction so no one could pray to another god. They didn't say everyone had to worship King Darius, just refrain from any other prayer. Yet Daniel wouldn't even do that. He wouldn't pray in silence or obscurity. He wouldn't camouflage his efforts or offer partial obedience. He chose blatant, unconcealed, deliberate faithfulness to God.

Perhaps in hopefulness, he opened his window and prayed toward Solomon's temple in Jerusalem. It stood when he was taken as a boy. It currently sat in ashes, as he well knew. I'm sure he recalled Solomon's words when he dedicated the temple to God, recounted over the years:

May your eyes be open toward this temple night and day, this place of which you said, "My Name shall be there," so that you will hear the prayer your servant prays toward this place. Hear the supplication of your servant and of your people Israel when they pray toward this place. (1 Kings 8:29-30)

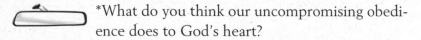 *Have you ever just needed to go back to where God has always been for you? Where is that? A place? A memory? A relationship? Why is it special?

Verse 11 is critical because "these men went as a group and found Daniel praying and asking God for help." In utter obedience, Daniel summoned God. He wasn't in the closet or under his covers. He was in plain view, displaying his loyalty for all to witness, asking the object of his affection for help. This was a man who needed a word from heaven, and he asked for it in the context of his own faithfulness. Not just that day, but all the 24,455 days he'd been in Babylon.

*What do you think our uncompromising obedience does to God's heart?

It certainly prompts Him to move on our behalf, speak to us. For all God has done, He only asks for our love. When given freely, there is nothing God won't do for His people. If you want to see Him move in your life, become radically obedient, and watch out.

Read Daniel 6:12-23. List every benefit of Daniel's obedience to God you can find in these verses.

Girls, how is your obedience level? Would people look at your life and find a woman who serves God continually? Take quick inventory on the convictions of the Holy Spirit:

- How are you doing on loving God with all your heart?
- How about loving your neighbor as much as your own life?
- Are you spending time in His Word?
- Are you letting God deal with your sin?
- Have you obeyed the last thing He asked of you?

To accomplish this work in our lives, God gives us the Holy Spirit, who brings conviction. It's His way of putting up a hedge of protection when we're about to derail. We often view convictions as restrictive, but they are protective. They also point us toward the good paths God has planned for us and steer us toward God's work.

The Spirit's voice of conviction is about my favorite thing to hear. It reminds me that God cares about the direction I'm going. Conviction makes me feel safe; He'll never let me go too far without warning me, in matters large and small. You know how to recognize it: It's that unshakeable pressure until you obey, whether for discipline or kingdom work, when you want to holler, "Okay! I get it!" And, as we read in Week One, the Spirit's voice doesn't argue with you or try to convince you. He just speaks, and you know what to do.

How do you typically respond to conviction? Favorably? Reluctantly? (It might help to think of a particular situation.) Has conviction gone unanswered in your life for so long you no longer hear it? (If you can't think of a situation, that in itself says something.)

Those five convictions of the Spirit seem basic, but if you work on them, you'll have to turn the volume down on God's voice just to get some sleep at night. And even then, He may wake you up to talk. He speaks to this believer because she does what He says. Doesn't that make sense? Those conversations are productive, not an exercise in futility. God doesn't have time to waste, so He seeks the faithful. Not the perfect, the faithful. Be the one He seeks. Be the one He blesses. Be the one He can count on. And you'll be the one who hears Him.

I issue a decree that in every part of my kingdom people must fear and reverence the God of Daniel.

For he is the living God
  and he endures forever;
his kingdom will not be destroyed,
  his dominion will never end.
He rescues and he saves;
  he performs signs and wonders
    in the heavens and on the earth.
He has rescued Daniel
  from the power of the lions. (Daniel 6:26-27)

Spend some time evaluating your obedience today with the help of the Spirit. Ask God if there is something He has asked of you that He's still waiting for. If you are willing, commit to radical obedience to the best of your abilities in the five areas listed earlier.

Humility

Most of what we've studied boils down to two things: (1) knowing God deeper makes His voice more recognizable, and (2) by our choices we can become the women God speaks to. There is no shortcut. There is no trickery. Deepening our relationship (which magnifies our communication) with the Lord requires much from us.

Today focuses on the second component: becoming the ones God speaks to. Rather than feeling overwhelmed by that, be encouraged, Girls. Despite all the godly communication factors that are entirely out of your hands, this one you can control. You can't box in God's voice or reduce it to a formula. You can't force Him to speak or decide how His words should be delivered. But you *can* present yourself as a woman who wants to hear from Him. As much as it depends on you, you can be ready to listen.

Daniel was a shining example in this area. He exercised faithfulness, used his gifts for God's glory, spent time in His presence, and lived with integrity. In return, God spoke so clearly to him that the writing was literally on the wall (see Daniel 5). When the Lord looked down on Daniel and asked,

"What good would it do me to speak to him?" the answer was a resounding, "Much good. He can be counted on."

In the same year God rescued Daniel from the lion's den, he was given a vision of the restoration of Judah, Jesus' coming, the second destruction of Jerusalem in AD 70, and the end times. Talk about an earful. So let's back up just a bit and see what prompted this strong word from heaven.

Read Daniel 9:1-3. Which of the formats that we've already studied do you see Daniel engaging in to hear God?

Jeremiah was his older contemporary (now deceased), yet Daniel regarded his prophesies highly enough to refer to them as "the Scriptures." We find Daniel poring over Scripture even though he was a top official for one of the greatest monarchs on earth. His prestige never trumped his faith. He was a man who studied God's Word—even before it was completely fulfilled or packaged in leather. He read a prophecy Jeremiah had written in a letter from Jerusalem to the exiles in Babylon:

> This is what the Lord says: "When seventy years are completed for Babylon, I will come to you and fulfill my gracious promise to bring you back to this place. For I know the plans I have for you," declares the Lord, "plans to prosper you and not to harm you, plans to give you hope and a future." (Jeremiah 29:10-11)

Daniel did the math. Sixty-eight, sixty-nine. . . . Oh my land. Their exile was almost up, according to God. Discerningly, Daniel understood that it was their rebellion that landed them in Babylon in the first place. Captivity was God's way of bringing His people back into the fold. It was the tool by which they were purged of idolatry and irreverence. Daniel knew it was time for extreme repentance (that's why he fasted) and submission to the discipline God ordained. As Matthew Henry noted, "When the day of deliverance dawns it is time for God's praying people to bestir themselves; something extraordinary is then expected and required from them, besides their daily sacrifice."[2]

It was time for humility.

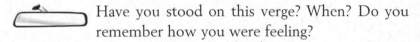 Read Daniel 9:4-19. Why do you think Daniel identified himself with his nation's sins even though he'd lived a long life of righteousness?

*How does Daniel show humility in this passage?

It's a beautiful place to stand: at the end of captivity on the cusp of God's restoration, when His work has been accomplished and His discipline has produced a harvest of righteousness (see Hebrews 12:11). The clouds start to part, and just when it seemed you might never smile again, life returns. The blanket of oppression begins to lift, and you take a deep breath for the first time. Freedom is within your reach.

Have you stood on this verge? When? Do you remember how you were feeling?

*Why do you think God requires our humility as we emerge from captivity into restoration?

Of course, a hundred other attitudes threaten to surface at that point:

- "Thanks for nothing, God. That was pretty much the worst season of my life."
- "How could You have let that happen to me?"
- "Where were You?"

Or perhaps the darkness of captivity overwhelmed with such force, you went numb. Sometimes you cry until you're dry and there's nothing left but blankness. Captivity often renders us not only empty, but blind. In many cases, we are unable to see our ownership in the captivity that besieged us. Darkness often comes on the heels of rebellion, yet God becomes the scapegoat. That same blindness shields our eyes from the righteousness God produced out of the darkness. We don't want to see that; we're too devastated.

 *Has any of that happened to you? If so, when?

Believer, no one wants liberty for you more than God. When it becomes time to walk back into the light, God brings His army of angels in full force to usher you back into freedom.

Read Daniel 9:20-23. If Gabriel was sent to deliver a word to Daniel at the *start* of his prayer, what do you think moved God to answer? It couldn't have been Daniel's words, because he'd just begun praying.

Girls, we must put on humility as a garment that covers us from head to toe. Empty words of submission will fall on deaf ears. In fact, humility goes well beyond words, as Daniel's communion with God demonstrates. It's an attitude of the heart, and it compels our King to answer us in stunning fashion.

Humility is looking toward heaven through tears, through bone weariness, and thanking Him for the freedom that's coming. It's owning the sin that robbed you of your liberty and repenting of it, face down. Humility identifies every goodness God was able to work in spite of captivity, maybe because of it. It names them one by one and digs deep to find thankfulness, even though the lessons were costly.

Even when captivity is entirely our fault, God can use it

for righteousness and restored fellowship. He can truly wrestle water out of a rock. Look what seventy years in Babylon did for the Jews: *

- They were almost completely cured of idolatry. Captivity taught them to abhor the worship of idols, and it was almost a nonissue for the rest of their history.
- The order of "scribes" was instituted to preserve the Scriptures, because the people were isolated from Jerusalem and the temple. The scribes in turn produced the rabbinical literature known as the Talmud and penned parts of the Old Testament we read today.
- Synagogues were instituted in captivity to preserve worship and religious education. They were so effective, the Jews built them when they returned to Judah, and synagogues ultimately made faith accessible to all Jews. Our Savior taught in synagogues, and the early church spread through them.
- The Jewish people pursued the Scriptures with new fervency. With their temple and city burned, they clung to God's Word, the only thing they had left. Ezra recounts their new passion for the Scriptures upon their return.
- Because of captivity, the Jewish people returned united and purified. Their commonalities and shared sufferings produced a spirit of unity unmatched before.[3]

*Think back to a season of captivity in your life. What good was God able to work through it? Even when someone has harmed you, you can thank God for the good without saying that what the other person did was okay or "for the best."

This is what God is listening for. It doesn't matter if your actual words are beautiful like Daniel's or nothing more than a series of phrases and sobs. If they are offered in humility, He is on His way to you. If you are in a season of darkness or on the verge of freedom, Believer, put on humility before God and let His mercy rain down until you feel the warm sunshine of freedom once again.

As soon as you began to pray, an answer was given. (Daniel 9:23)

Humility is hard. Ask the Spirit to help you release any bitterness, anger, or pride that stands in the way. Pray for sweet submission to win in your heart.

Tune In

Daniel remained in Babylon until his death, but his people were restored to Jerusalem as God promised. No doubt Daniel's counsel in the ears of the kings influenced them to treat the Jews respectfully while in captivity, as well as return them to their home.

God used Daniel to bring His power into a godless land. King Nebuchadnezzar declared, "Surely your God is the God of gods and the Lord of kings and a revealer of mysteries" (Daniel 2:47). King Darius proclaimed, "I issue a decree that in every part of my kingdom people must fear and reverence the God of Daniel. For he is the living God and he endures forever" (6:26). Out of the mouths of enemies came praises of the Living God.

This story fulfilled prophecy that the Jews would be in captivity to Babylon for seventy years. It began officially in 586 BC when:

- Jerusalem, including its walls, gates, and temple, was burned to the ground.

- The final wave of Jews was deported.
- The last Judean king was tortured and imprisoned (ending the monarchy), and Israel as a self-governing nation ceased to exist.

The captivity officially ended in 516 BC when the returned captives finished rebuilding the temple. Seventy years exactly. God is always right. If fulfilled prophecy doesn't give you goose bumps, you need to check for a pulse.

Let's study a psalm of celebration sung as the captives returned eight hundred miles across the Arabian Desert to Jerusalem after all those years in captivity. Before we begin, pray for insight into God's Word today. Ask the Spirit to teach you truth.

Remember, this is not a list of questions to answer. These are simply suggestions on how to interact with Scripture. Use any, springboard off one, or work through each passage on your own. After reading, spend a few minutes allowing the Spirit to talk to you. What is He saying? What do you see? Write your thoughts down in your journal as you go.

Read Psalm 126:1-2.

- Zion (Jerusalem) never looked so good. There's nothing like captivity to make you appreciate what you once had. Do you need to find renewed appreciation for the Zion you're in? Maybe the Zion you've returned to?
- Has your mouth ever been filled with laughter by God's deliverance? Did you have to laugh out loud?
- Has God fulfilled your wildest dreams through His mercy? When? What did He do that you wanted so badly?
- When has God's relationship with you caused others to acknowledge His love for you? What great things did He do that attracted the notice of others?

Read Psalm 126:3-4.

- They found joy on the heels of devastation. Can you? Why or why not?
- They returned to a burned-down city, Solomon's glorious temple destroyed. How do you think they prayed post-captivity? What had they learned?
- The Negev was a dry desert. Is this you, Believer? Has heartache left you parched? Bring that before God. Tell Him where you're at.
- The streams in the Negev ran bone-dry in the summer, but the winter rains renewed their flow and they came to life. Do you need restoration like the streams in the Negev? Jesus is Living Water. Ask Him to saturate your thirsty heart. Be open to receive Him.

Read Psalm 126:5-6.

- Humility often requires us to sow in tears. Do you do this? Is repentance natural or hard for you? Why?
- God's history shows that He delivers joy to His people who've humbled themselves in tears. Why does one have to come before the other? Is there something specific you need to humble yourself about?
- Are you in a season of planting? Is the hard work you're enduring in preparation for a harvest? Ask God to reveal this to you. What is He getting you ready for?
- Are you on the other side in a season of harvest? Yeah for you! Where has God brought you? Can you look back and see His hand all along?

God is ultimately a God of freedom. He strains toward it.

He urges each of us to live in it. After all, "it is for freedom that Christ has set us free" (Galatians 5:1). This is why we must put on humility and wrap ourselves in obedience. It's why we heed the Holy Spirit's warnings as He protects us from the dangers of our wanderings. It's why we run into the arms of our spiritual gifts, staying on task. Those are all His efforts to keep us in Zion, far from the oppression of captivity. He works hard to keep us safe.

And you know why, right? Imagine how He feels to look down from heaven and find His treasured people, whose mouths are filled with laughter, living their dreams and shouting for joy. That's what He created us for.

Then it was said among the nations, "The LORD has done great things for them" (Psalm 126:2).

He Speaks Through Circumstances

[JOB]

Spiritual Warfare

My husband and I produced two boys, ages seven and three, and one priss, age five. When I hear arguments for "nature versus nurture," I laugh out loud. My boys made guns out of pancakes when they could barely talk. In our household, there is much wrestling, karate, punching, and general combat among the males. Apparently this is fun, and I'd like to see the mother who thinks she could stop it.

But our daughter is about the biggest princess that ever lived, and she rarely gets in on the "fun." However, she occasionally eyes the battlefield longingly and decides to join the warfare with her brothers. At this point, my husband and I begin the countdown: "Five, four, three, two. . . ." We rarely make it to one before she's crying on the sidelines, wounded from battle.

She buries her defeated head in my shoulder and wails, "The boys fight me too hard, Mama! They don't even *try* to fight gentle!" I try not to laugh and pray my daughter's skin thickens substantially before she hits the teen years with two mean brothers. I'm not prepared for the drama that surely awaits me.

We girls generally prefer the sidelines. All-out war is rarely appealing to God's princesses. Can't we all just get along? Can't the world be a place of rainbows and butterflies? I wish it could be, but frankly, we're living in a minefield. Life on this earth as a believer is war. We have an Enemy who fights us hard—he doesn't even try to fight gentle. God considers this battle far more than we do. In fact, He has much to say about it and through it. We must listen for His voice as He guides us through spiritual warfare.

This week we're going to study one of the hardest stories in the Bible: Job's. We'll discover some ways God speaks through circumstances. It's good that He does, because they constantly frame our lives. Something is always going on: a challenge, a victory, a heartbreak, a season of one kind or another. And we're always trying to find God in all of them.

So did Job, bless him. Before we begin, there is critical context we need to establish. I know the book of Job appears smack in the middle of the Old Testament, but its events actually took place near the beginning of the biblical period. The setting appears to have been somewhere between 2100–1700 BC, just before or after the patriarchs of Genesis. Scholars estimate these dates by several factors:

- Job lived over 140 years, a lifespan similar to the Hebrew patriarchs (see 42:16).
- His wealth was measured in cattle (see 1:3), not in money.
- He acted as priest for his family (see 1:5).
- The raiding of the Sabean and Chaldean tribes fits the second millennium BC (see 1:15,17).
- There is no mention of covenant or law as established through Moses.[1]

What this tells us is that Job lived when faith was in its most primitive form. He had no Scriptures to consult, no national history to reference, no God-appointed leadership to learn from, no temple to worship in. What he knew of God was a fraction of what we are privileged to know today.

So as we read, keep in mind that Job deals with our relationship with God in a rudimentary fashion. We see the account of a non-Jewish tribal family, patriarchal in nature, in an underdeveloped territory east of the Jordan River. Think *beginning of history*.

Read Job 1:1-5. From this text, what can you gather about Job's feelings toward God? His understanding of Him and their relationship?

When I realize that Job had nothing to go on, his knowledge of God seems advanced. He followed some principles of dealing with God that weren't introduced for another five hundred years when the law was detailed to Moses. Though Job's perspective was limited, it was an exact precursor to God's future word. There was nothing contradictory in his understanding; it was just primitive.

*How does this speak to the age-old question, "What about the village people in Africa who've never been witnessed to?"

Read Job 1:6-8. How would you characterize Satan's reply in verse 7? Do you interpret his answer as vicious? Calculating? Taunting? Bored? What do you see?

Perhaps he came baiting God, airing his victories as he terrorized the earth he'd been confined to. "I've been roaming back and forth throughout the earth, and I've taken many casualties. The people belong to me. Your precious creation is entirely corrupted." Then God tempered his arrogance by reminding him of Job, His faithful servant.

Or maybe Satan came with Job in mind all along, as God would have known. "I've been roaming this earth, going back and forth. I've got my sights set on your so-called servant. He's raising a godly family and damaging my progress." To which God replied, "Have you *considered* my servant Job? He's entirely upright, and he loves me. You've chosen a poor target."

If Satan asked permission to test your faith, what do you think God would say about you?

Read Job 1:9-12. How did Satan try to destroy God's pleasure in Job?

On a larger scale, what was Satan trying to prove about our relationship with God?

Girls, before the war broke out in Job's backyard, it was begun in heaven. Job's struggle was ultimately between our King and His Enemy. If the godliness of the righteous man in whom God delighted could be exposed as sinful, selfish, *insincere*, then a chasm of alienation stood between them that could never be bridged. Even redemption would be beyond reach, because the "greatest man among all the people" would be revealed as the most ungodly, using the Lord only for his own prosperity. God's whole enterprise in creation and redemption would be shown as radically flawed, one big sham.[2]

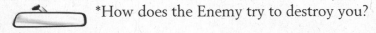 *How does the Enemy try to destroy you?

What do you think he tries to convince God about you?

Girls, Satan is after us. He doesn't fight fair. He hits below the belt. His goal is ultimate destruction of life, of health, of faith. Not only does he plan on devastating the life of every individual, but her family, her witness, and ultimately, her loyalty to God. In turn, Satan longs to discourage the King. He can't wait to point to a life in ruins and say, "See, she never really loved You. At the first sign of trouble, she cursed You."

So what does this have to do with hearing God? It's time to heed His shouts of warning. He speaks through warfare. Both our Lord and the Enemy know our most vulnerable areas. Spiritual battles often take us by surprise, because we're not ready. We haven't shored up our defenses. Satan looked at Job and knew just what to attack: his prosperity. Job showed his cards when he said, "What I feared has come upon me; what I dreaded has happened to me" (3:25). The Enemy preyed on his biggest fear: losing his stuff.

He looks at you and knows exactly where to attack, too. He has many weapons in his arsenal: shame, bitterness, pride, despair, blame, anger, complacency, lust, guilt, self-loathing. For some, he takes their despair and applies it to their marriage: "There is no hope." For others, he uses their self-loathing against their own image: "Everyone is disappointed in you, including God." Satan takes you into full account and determines how to lead you astray.

Girls, God is not silent while our Enemy attacks! It is imperative that we tune in to His instruction, His battle plan to keep us safe. Not only does He identify the areas Satan will most likely attack, but He speaks perfect strategies on how to defend ourselves.

*Consider a personal spiritual battle, either past or present. Through it, what area of weakness in you is God pointing out?

*How is He telling you to fight off the Enemy? What are your specific instructions? (Don't know? Ask. Look in His Word.)

Spiritual warfare is often an indicator of God's plan to use you in the near future. Do you think He's getting you ready for something? Has He been preparing you for a task? A mission? What makes you say that?

Of course, God allowed Satan to take everything from Job except his life. And to that, we scratch our heads, get mad. We'll talk about that tomorrow, but remember what was at stake: the entire premise that a person can be devoted to God regardless of prosperity. Satan was trying to discredit the possibility of sincere love by believers.

Nothing has changed.

A battle rages on. Just because you're not listening for it doesn't mean it's not happening. If Satan can cut your legs out while you're coasting in complacency, even better. Then he can point a finger in God's face and mock your relationship.

Girls, let's stand up collectively in the midst of our spiritual battles and declare that we serve a King of Kings who will ultimately be victorious. Let's shout out our devotion for Him to silence the taunts of His Enemy. We can still cry. We can grieve and mourn. But we'll still love our Lord and honor the sacrifice that brought us into His presence with sincere hearts. The Enemy may bend us, but he won't break us. We wouldn't give him the satisfaction.

We will shout for joy when you are victorious
   and will lift up our banners in the name of our God.
      (Psalm 20:5)

Do you need a fresh awareness of the battle for your soul? God is urging you to listen. Ask Him what areas need to be strengthened in your life. Ask if He's preparing you for something. Pray for the opportunities to prove your love for Him in the midst of battle. Be God's trophy.

Suffering

You know when you have a confrontation coming, and you couldn't dread it more? It must take place, but you lose sleep over it. I kind of feel like that as I write this day of study. Perhaps in preparation for these pages, God surrounded me with friends and family who have suffered this year: death, infertility, marriages, careers, relationships, even lost honor.

Suffering is such a difficult topic. It's hard to understand, deal with, work through, counsel, endure. It's awful for the sufferers. It's painful for those of us who love them. We want to explain it, give it a godly context that will alleviate the pain or lessen the damage. We pore over Scripture trying to make sense of it, but often we erroneously rub salt in open wounds:

"It'll get better. God will work it out. Don't worry."
"This is just the way God must have wanted it."
"Don't get angry at God."
"He must be disciplining you."

Though his story happened long ago, Job shows us that things have changed entirely, and they haven't changed at all.

Job's suffering sent his friends and him into such a tailspin, they didn't know which way was up.

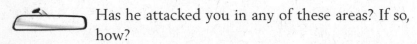 Read Job 1:13-22. When Job said "The LORD gave and the LORD has taken away" (verse 21), how accurate was this statement? Based on verse 12, would you say the Lord had taken away? Why or why not?

Allowing calamity and *causing* calamity are two different things. It has been the nature of man since the beginning to lay all suffering at God's feet. We declare Him angry or mean or unsearchable. We conclude that if bad things happen, it must be God's doing. How else could it be?

It could be that we have a vicious Enemy. This Enemy is the one who took Job's servants, his cattle, his children—not God. He is not an adversary to take lightly. He is altogether vicious. We read this account of Job and it takes our breath away.

But what is so different?

He brutalizes our livelihood by attacking our education early, our careers later. Satan has cast a black pallor of death over our entire country in terms of financial carnage, unmanageable debt. The Enemy steals our children to this day, killing their integrity, their purity, their innocence. He robs our bodies of health and tempts us toward destructive physical habits. His battle plan has been the same since the beginning of time.

Has he attacked you in any of these areas? If so, how?

*Why do you think God allows this?

*How do you think we should view a God who allows this?

Read Job 2:1-10. Why do you think Satan saved this attack for last?

Believer, have you ever found yourself sitting in ashes, scraping your wounds in misery? That place where, as far as you can imagine, life couldn't be worse? If you're there, Friend, I pray you hear a strong word from God today. I won't try to explain away your suffering or give it a false spin. I walk with you as a friend who loves you, and my only desire is that God's Word envelopes you to bestow on you "a crown of beauty instead of ashes, the oil of gladness instead of mourning" (Isaiah 61:3).

In case you're starting to think Job set an impossible standard with all his worship and praising and apparent lack of emotion, let's turn a few pages.

Read Job 6:11-17. What agonies of suffering do you see in Job? What questions did he ask that we still ask today?

Upon hearing of Job's suffering, his three friends came to "comfort" him. They should've kept their day jobs. With friends like these, who needs Satan? Now, God love 'em, they also had a limited understanding of the Lord. They tried their best based on what they thought they knew. Regardless, we can't study Job and accept his friends' counsel as completely accurate. Certainly they contained elements of truth, but as we read later, "[The Lord] said to Eliphaz the Temanite, 'I am angry with you and your two friends, because you have not spoken of me what is right, as my servant Job has'" (42:7). In fact, God called their counsel "folly" (42:8).

Here's why. What did each of his friends erroneously attribute Job's suffering to?

Bildad: Job 8:1-4

Zophar: Job 20:4-7

Eliphaz: Job 22:4-11

Here is a summary of their twenty-eight-chapter dialogue:

"You're full of sin, Job."
"No, I'm not."
"You must be."
"I'm innocent."
"It's got to be your fault."
"It's not."
"Is."
"Not."

Read Job's reply in 27:1-6. Even though defending his integrity, what conflict do you see between his emotions and his faith (verse 2)?

I know it's hard, Believer. When losses overwhelm and despair envelopes us, affection for God is elusive. No matter what we've learned about suffering through His Word, the pain remains. Yet in Job's story, God communicates such a freedom to us as we suffer, I want to be sure you hear it today.

God declared that, throughout all his ranting, raving, screaming, and sobbing, Job had spoken right of Him (see 42:8). *What?* This can't be right. Job cursed the day he was born and begged for death. He abandoned all hope and concluded that God's hand was against him. His despair was so palpable, we cry for his misery four thousand years later.

Oh, Girls, God is telling us that He allows us to cry when we're suffering. He lets us lie on the ground and scream and wail. He patiently endures our anger, knowing we don't understand. We can yell, "It's not fair!" He allows that emotion. There is a time to weep and mourn (see Ecclesiastes 3:4). He doesn't judge our fragility or despise our devastation. We were made in His image, created for real emotion. Cry, Believer. You are not required to put on an air of indifference while you suffer.

But hear this: Job ranted, and he mischaracterized God something fierce, assuming incorrectly that God's hand was against him. *But* he never turned his back on God or cursed him, though his wife encouraged him to. He never deserted his faith. He poorly concluded that God had abandoned him, but he'd just as soon die than speak against Him (see 6:9-10). He certainly didn't have warm fuzzy feelings toward God, but reverence is not a feeling. It's a choice. You can feel confused, sad, even furious toward God and still maintain respect.

*Do you need to hear that today? What is God telling you about your own suffering?

Suffering offends our sense of justice, just as it did Job. When outside our own control, it seems unfair, completely undeserved. How could God let bad stuff happen when we're trying so hard to live for Him?

Job felt that same way, yet we're given the privilege of perspective: Satan had challenged the sincerity of man's relationship with God. Job's suffering had a noble purpose, although he was unaware of it.

Believer, what was fair about our perfect Savior hanging sinless on a cross? There was never a moment when suffering was more undeserved. What if Jesus had declared, "It's not fair! I won't endure it!" Surely His followers felt the same. The lies brought against Him, false testimony that condemned Him, assaulted their notion of God's justice. Where was He? How could He allow His Son to die unjustly? Peter even declared, "Never, Lord!. . . . This shall never happen to you!" (Matthew 16:22).

If they knew then what we know now.

In your history with God, has He ever accomplished good through your suffering?

In the hands of God, suffering can be transformed into salvation, pain into prosperity. There are times when the latter can overwhelm the former by no other means. He allows it for that reason. Does that lessen our pain? Does it mean we wish to suffer? No. Nor does He expect that emotion from us. He can absorb our anger as long as it is wrapped in our reverence.

The LORD said to Job: . . .
"Would you discredit my justice?
    Would you condemn me to justify yourself?
Do you have an arm like God's,
    and can your voice thunder like his?" (40:1,8-9)

Then Job replied to the LORD:
"I know that you can do all things;
    no plan of yours can be thwarted. . . .
Surely I spoke of things I did not understand,
    things too wonderful for me to know." (42:1-3)

Part of understanding God's communication is knowing not just how He talks, but how He listens. If you need to pour out grief and scream before Him today, do it. He allows it. Let Him love you, comfort you. Keep your reverence in check, and He can transform ashes into wonderful things.

Discipline

I hate to be wrong. Hate. It. I'm a firstborn, which sent surges of flawed DNA through my veins that require me to be right. When the DNA gets challenged, it betrays my body by causing my neck to turn blotchy. It even overtakes my vocal cords and compels me to blurt out ugly sentiments in a high voice. If the DNA doesn't get its way, it forces my voice even higher and double-times my speech like an auctioneer:

Whatdoyoumeanyoudisagree? Iloveyoubutyou'rewrong.
It'sveryobviousthatI'mright.Howcouldyoueventhinkthat?
Trustme,Iknow.
CanIgeta"You'reright,Jen?"
Goingonce,goingtwice, soldtothemanwhosebeenworndown
fortwelve
yearsbyanopinionatedwifewhoisneverwrong!

What can I do? It's the DNA.

This arrangement has failed to work out between God and me. Evidently, there are times when I am, in fact, wrong, and God is required to call me on it. Furthermore, I am subjected to suffering the consequences of my wrongness and have even had a few privileges revoked until I played nice. The DNA obviously has a hard time bending its stubborn pride to this type of correction, but I try to reason with it as best I can: "It's for your own good. He's only trying to protect you. Stop getting so blotchy."

Discipline. As parents, we totally get it. As children of God, we can't stand it. We want to hear nice things from God, such as "You're a beautiful princess, and I adore every single thing you do." These sentiments work for us. It's much less pleasant to get called out on our bad behavior and unhealthy habits. And to be broken of them? Ouch. There are certain areas we'd rather keep to ourselves, thank you very much.

But of all the methods God uses to speak to us, discipline is one of the most imperative. We must learn to turn an ear to discipline, listen to what God is saying through it, and allow it to produce righteousness in our lives.

In Job's story, his three friends talked themselves silly. Their arguments against him ran out of steam, and I'm sure they needed oxygen after their wordy lectures, er, I mean comfort. Poor Job cried, "Miserable comforters are you all! Will your long-winded speeches never end?" (16:2-3). When their charges against him were finally suffocated by Job's protestations of innocence, a fourth counselor joined the scene.

Meet Elihu. Read Job 32:1-12. For what did he blame Job? For what did he blame Job's friends?

I'll be honest: I like Elihu. I think he was a scrapper. Oh sure, he was a young whippersnapper by comparison, but it is at this point we finally see someone get it mostly right; neither misjudging God nor Job. God thought so too, as only the other three were reprimanded for their poor counsel. In his rebuke of Job, Elihu never falsely accused his earlier life but confined his criticism to how Job misunderstood God.

*Read Job 33:12-14. Land sakes! He's teaching this study! Why do you think suffering often hinders us from hearing God's voice?

Elihu went on to demonstrate a specific way God speaks to His people: discipline. Unlike the other three, Elihu didn't claim God was currently disciplining Job for a sinful life. Elihu simply proved to Job that God did, indeed, speak. In other words, how could Job charge God with silence when so many others could attest to His clear voice of discipline? In fact, when one warning is ignored, God issues another by a different means (33:14).

Read Job 33:15-22. God will bring you to the edge of death to preserve your soul. Why is this hard for us to accept, much less appreciate?

Matthew Henry said, "See what a mercy it is to be under the restraints of an awakened conscience. Faithful are the wounds, and kind are the bonds, of that friend, for by them the soul is kept from perishing eternally."[3] Girls, if correction seems harsh, imagine life without it. Like undisciplined children, we become victims of our own immaturity, putting ourselves in constant danger. We become unmanageable, unreasonable. Left unchecked, our rebellion removes us from the protection of our Father. We wake up one day to find ourselves in a foreign country, broke, destitute, empty, wishing for the slop of pigs like the prodigal son.

To spare you from that, the Spirit throws up roadblocks in your soul. He removes your peace and presses on your uneasiness. He'll allow your sin to wreak its consequences without buffering them for you. The Spirit moves in your heart with such clarity, you are certain of the destructive path you are either on or approaching. It becomes only a matter of obedi-ence for you. It is impossible to find yourself at the end of that road lamenting, "I had no idea! God didn't warn me!"

*How has God disciplined you? (Has He removed a relationship? Put up a boundary where you didn't want it? Let you suffer the full effects of your own sinful choices?)

What was He sparing you from?

Read Job 33:23-30. Though this occurred at the beginning of biblical history, where do you see Jesus in this passage?

God communicates through discipline because He loves us too much to let our own sin destroy us. It is not out of anger, as we often interpret it. It is out of desperate love for the work of His hands. It's the same urgency that compels you to scream at the top of your lungs and fiercely discipline your child when she runs into a busy street, as your heart pounds out of your chest at the mere possibility of losing her. You may come across as angry, but if only she knew the source of your emotion. If she only knew how you cried for days just recall-ing that moment. Our children have no concept of our fierce love for them.

From that perspective, have you ever misunder-stood God's discipline? Have you ever mishan-dled it? How?

Elihu paved the way for God to finally speak. He declared the Lord as present, not absent; just, not unfair; loving, not cruel. I'd say the young fella nailed it. After listening to Job and his friends spin their yarns, God interceded after Elihu brought them back to center.

The narrator tells us, "Then the LORD answered Job out of the storm" (38:1). Can you imagine how they freaked out? Remember, this was way before any burning bushes or pillars of fire or any famous instances of God speaking out loud. Elihu had just said, "God's voice thunders in marvelous ways; he does great things beyond our understanding" (37:5), but he was only trying to sound pretty, not give God any ideas! Yet the storm gathered, the sky darkened, and God's voice thundered from the clouds. I want to cover my face just thinking about it.

Like Elihu, God proceeded to discipline Job for mischaracterizing Him. Though His lecture to Job reduces us to molecules, think how much worse it would have been had Job cursed Him!

*Read a bit of it in Job 38:1-21. Holy cow. Why do you think God answered Job like this rather than directly answering his many questions? Why not explain about Satan's challenge? What can we learn from this?

There are times when the reason for our suffering is veiled. Do we want to accept that? Of course not. I heard a brilliant statement from a pastor addressing this conflict: "Sometimes you have to let God be God and let your mind suffer."

Doesn't God's reply to Job seem to support that? Job's trials had a divine purpose, yet it wasn't revealed to relieve his confusion. Instead God said, "I am God. You are not." Strangely enough, it was sufficient for Job, though we'd swear he of all people would require answers. We can only infer that in God's discourse, Job saw the justice he had waited for. He heard the voice he thought had gone silent. He realized God loved him; He had never despised him. In the absence of an indictment, God upheld Job's innocence. And it was enough.

To that, Job replied: "My ears had heard of you but now my eyes have seen you. Therefore I despise myself and repent in dust and ashes" (42:5-6).

What did God's discipline produce in Job's life?

Girls, let's listen to God's discipline. Rather than stiffening our necks or demanding answers, let's bend a knee to God's sovereignty. When He says "No," may we release what we're gripping so tightly. When He draws a boundary or removes a vice, let's submit to His authority; He knows better than we do. In every instance, may we remember that He loves us with a desperate love, He'll do anything to keep us safe, and He lives to preserve our souls.

> He is wooing you from the jaws of distress
>   to a spacious place free from restriction,
>   to the comfort of your table laden with choice
>   food. (36:16)

What has God spoken to you in discipline recently? Have you obeyed? Ask the Spirit to reveal God's hedge of protection around you. Pray to understand it as an extension of His passion for you.

Peace

Forty-two is my favorite number. I take one look at a four followed by a two, and I want to dance. I'd like to commemorate my 4-2 affection by spending forty-two dollars on a pair of shoes; better yet, purchase forty-two pairs of shoes. I'd consider a "42" tattoo, but there is not a decent area left on my body. It's all been ravaged by childbirth and irresponsible tanning. I'd settle for forty-two days in Europe, but it would all have to go on credit cards at 42 percent interest, robbing our children of their college fund and ensuring they'd live with us for forty-two straight months after graduation to pay off their Stafford loans. So for now, I'll just enjoy my favorite number quietly.

Forty-two.

As in, Job chapter 42.

Sweet God, thank You for chapter 42. Thank You for bringing this tragedy full circle and delivering restoration. Chapter 42 overtakes the bitterness of chapters 1–41, and for that we are grateful. Girls, let's learn about one more circumstance God speaks through: peace.

Having thundered for four straight chapters to put Job in his place (and to put the kibosh on his friends' pious lecturing), God finally let Job turn the corner.

Read Job 42:7-9. Have you ever been on the receiving end of poor counsel during suffering? Have you ever been a poor counselor? When?

In order to understand the peace God administered, we have to acknowledge the crux of this struggle. Remember, Satan challenged God on His crowning vision for all creation: relationship. He didn't attack the earth or animals. He didn't mock God's timing or creativity. As he does with us, Satan attacked what was nearest to God's heart: sincere intimacy with His people.

There could be no celebration of chapter 42 had Job cursed God and abandoned their relationship. If the "greatest man among all the people" loved God conditionally, only if his life prospered, then Satan would have won that day. He would have laughed in God's face and declared humanity the Lord's biggest failure. He'd have thrown Job's betrayal at God's feet and mocked the very idea that a human would ever be loyal to Him outside of good fortune. At the very beginning of biblical history, Job's faithfulness secured the possibility for redemption. He silenced the lying mouth of hell.

In the midst of Job's suffering, read his words in 19:25-27. How do you imagine Satan felt when he heard that?

How do you think God felt?

Here we see peace that transcended suffering. Job had this peace in reserve. It had been established long before he suffered his first loss. When his prosperity went bankrupt, he was able to draw from a lifetime of God's faithfulness. Their history became Job's security. Though he rightly declared, "I have escaped with only the skin of my teeth" (19:20), he proclaimed five sentences later, "I know that my Redeemer lives!" (19:25). He cried, wailed, mourned, but God's peace preserved his conviction. It separated his faith from his fragile circumstances and kept it from destruction.

*Have you seen or experienced this phenomenon? How has God supernaturally activated His peace in your desperate circumstances?

We have to get our arms around that before we can enjoy the happy ending. Job's peace didn't begin in chapter 42. It was established long before we met him in chapter 1. Believer, if you want God to speak peace over your life, the moment of crisis is too late. You must know His voice in normality before you can recognize it in calamity. You can't draw from an empty well, and it is nearly impossible to fill your reserves in distress. When God's peace is a regular companion, it has the power to work when everyone around you says, "I don't know how she's even standing up." It's that powerful. Truly supernatural.

What does God say through peace?

Read Job 42:10-13. Sometimes peace transcends circumstances, and other times peace is administered through them. What did God communicate to Job over the course of this passage?

God's peace is a powerful communication tool. There are times when circumstances are firing on all cylinders. It seems doors are opening, prospects are abundant, the sun is shining. God has used those seasons to speak to me. He has cleared a path, removed all obstacles, and told me, "Run forward as quick as you can! You're in a good place." Everything feels right, the

Spirit within me confirms it, and an opportunity is effectively seized. Pleasant circumstances have a history of working well with humans. We love a good open door.

To test that word, we have the Spirit, because not every open door is one we should enter. There was an available boat with an affordable fee ready to set sail far from Nineveh, but that didn't mean God wanted Jonah to board that boat and run from his calling. You see what I'm saying?

Enter: peace. It's a fabulous tool for confirming circumstances. Simply put, the Spirit administers it liberally when we're on track, and He removes it when we're not. I love it. It's saved my hide more times than I can count. I call it "the peace factor." When it's in place, I make decisions with confidence. When it's missing, I want to crawl out of my skin.

*Has God ever led you through peace (or the absence of it)? If so, how?

Job's peace finally came down out of the stratosphere, high above his desperate circumstances, and cohabitated with them once again. God restored his fortune, doubling his animals and replacing his seven sons and three daughters. Here we often hit a snag in the happy ending: You can replace animals, health, even honor, but what about his children, God? He lost all ten of them. We don't want him to have new ones. We're still sad about the first set. That loss was beyond repair, and it often leaves us a little cold. I think God knew this would be hardest for us girls, because look how He inspired His Word:

Read Job 42:14-15. Considering the patriarchal world Job lived in, what strikes you as out of place in this passage? Why do you think this was included?

Believer, sometimes the blessing of a lifetime can only come on the heels of a loss. My friend lost her daughter tragically and after mourning decided to adopt a baby from another country. She recounted how she looked into her adopted daughter's face and understood the restoration of Job for the first time. She wouldn't have known her new child without losing the first. Of course, she would never have chosen the loss, but she learned the bittersweetness of Job's second reality. And she wouldn't have it any other way.

The second reality is part of life as a believer. We must lose our pride to gain salvation. Our agendas must die in favor of a life of submission. We sacrifice selfishness for holiness, pleasure for righteousness. Those are hard to lay down. We often miss them terribly. There is a comfort of God that only comes when we're in the dark. Though we wouldn't have chosen the trial, we wouldn't trade it for the sweet communion we experienced.

Believer, we are broken for godliness. The breaking, the setting, the healing is painful, but without it, we'd never stand up, straight and strong. Those who live in a second reality know it's true. Those who don't cannot imagine life beyond their first reality.

 *Do you have a second reality? If so, describe your circumstance.

God wanted us to know Job's second reality was a dandy. God gave Job peace for the rest of his long, healthy, happy life. In obedience, he lived in God's favor, enjoying his great-great grandchildren to the end of his days.

He even took pains to describe his lovely daughters, names and all. He named one *Keren-Happuch* meaning "container of antimony," a highly prized black powder used as eyeshadow to enlarge a woman's eyes and make them more attractive. To me, that's a little wink from heaven. Where black ashes once characterized Job's suffering, they later symbolized the beauty of his second reality fulfilled in his stunning daughter.

Beauty after ashes is more than possible. God is a God of chapter 42.

What kind of peace do you need God to speak to you? The kind of peace found in the dailiness of life? The kind that transcends suffering? The kind that restores your life? Ask the Spirit today to administer peace and fill your reserves as He leads you on.

Tune In

*T*he suffering of the godly will stand as one of the hardest questions of faith. Perhaps it's because we feel entitled to only happiness as children of God. Maybe it's because we make poor assumptions about God amid suffering, as Job did. Sometimes we have no concept of the cosmic struggle that mirrors our personal trial. Often it simply boils down to one thought: It's not fair.

Whether you are currently suffering, or you're walking with someone who is, let's take a closer look at some of Elihu's counsel today. His was the only advice God didn't reject. Let's see what we can learn about God and the suffering allowed on His watch.

Before you begin, please spend a few minutes in prayer. Ask God to remove your preconceived ideas and temper your anger. Pray for the Spirit to truly be your Teacher today. We can learn what we've never understood with His help.

Work through the following sections of Scripture, praying and journaling as you go. The questions provided are ones I'd ask of this passage. Feel free to use any of them, or respond differently if you choose. I hope you're learning how to really dissect and apply Scripture. God always answers good questions.

Read Job 36:1-7.

- Elihu found himself defending God to an angry Job. Is this your role to someone right now? Are you certain of God's goodness as Elihu was? Why or why not?
- Why do you think he said, "God is mighty, but does not despise men"? Why do we think one negates the other? How does that broaden your understanding of God?
- Do you believe suffering is a result of God being "firm in His purpose"? How does your history support that? Is hindsight a useful tool?
- What do you make of verse 7? How can you reconcile the pits of suffering with being enthroned with kings? How is this truth?

Read Job 36:8-12.

- If your chains are a result of sin, God wants you to know. "He tells them what they have done." Have you heard these words before? When? Is He speaking them now?
- How does verse 10 describe God's discipline? How does God accomplish His objective?
- Verse 11 in the *New American Standard Bible* says, "If they *hear* and serve Him . . . ." How's your ear toward discipline? Do you listen for it? Tune it out? Does your current reality indicate a life of peace born out of obedience or not?
- Those who ignore God's voice of discipline will "die without knowledge." What do you think that means?

Read Job 36:22-26.

- Have you declared to God, "You have done wrong"? It's okay to be honest. Have you tried to dictate His ways to Him? Why?
- In suffering, have you maintained reverence? Have you remembered to praise the work of His good hands? What does your answer reveal about your peace?
- Are you willing to sacrifice your understanding? Can you let God be God and let your mind suffer? Why is this hard?

Along with suffering, throw in predestination, the tribes in remote Africa, abuse of the innocent, epic natural disasters, and all other misery that is seemingly born out of injustice, and even a sturdy faith can be shaken. Girls, in my own journey of knowing God, He has brought me to a conclusion that has both educated and relieved me. After wrestling with God, losing years of my life trying to figure it all out, He spoke these words to me:

"I am justice."

Not only does God act justly, *He is justice*. It is not in His ability to act unfairly in any circumstance. He can no more act unjustly than He can lie. Believer, we simply cannot get our arms around divine justice that transcends our narrow perspective. I've rested knowing that even when I don't understand, *I believe God's justice*. I believe it more than I don't understand. When my limited knowledge has dissected a circumstance as much as it can and the questions remain, my confidence is secured in the certainty of God's fairness. I may not get it now, I may not get it ever, but I believe "He is mighty, and firm in his purpose." Those purposes extend beyond my boundaries. They are rooted in the very struggle of the ages, fulfilled outside my timeframe, which is but a breath. They are often distorted by sin and brutal attacks from the Enemy—not God. Give discredit where it's due.

The wrongs will be righted, if not in this life, in eternity.
His purposes will be accomplished.
He is always fair.
He is always right.

It is unthinkable that God would do wrong,
    that the Almighty would pervert justice. (Job 34:12)

Will you believe Him? Will you choose His knowledge over your own? Ask Him to speak to you. Beg for His life-giving words to bring you awareness, discipline, knowledge, and ultimately peace. He wants you to hear them.

WEEK SIX

God Haunts

Creation

As a freshman in college, I sojourned to a foreign place, a land of strangers, a region of peculiar people: Oklahoma. I was two-and-a-half hours from home, but a state line had been crossed, and it was like studying abroad. Bizarre language assaulted my ears daily. Strange places were discussed like "Chickasaw," "Konowa," and "Tahlequah." I was assaulted with abominations like honky-tonks and the OU Sooners. Not surprisingly, my first two friends were from Missouri. They didn't know how to Two-Step either.

It wasn't long and I began to miss home. I'd reached my threshold of ropers and cafeteria food. Plus, I'd run out of clean panties. I'd been gone two months, but it felt like two years. I'll never forget driving home. Every exit closer to home seemed like a familiar friend. Memorable landmarks declared I was almost there. I was never so happy to see the flat, ugly city of Wichita, Kansas. Mom cooked real food and washed my clothes. My friends got together and exchanged outrageous college stories—I mean, study tips. I was even glad to see my sisters.

It's good to go home.

We've spent several weeks discussing God's voice: ways He speaks, how to hear Him, how to develop our ears. But sometimes the best way to hear God's voice is to go where He is, where He has always been. Occasionally, we find ourselves in such foreign territory that going back to God's haunts is like coming home. We know He'll be there waiting for us. When we can't hear His voice any other way, we know where to find Him.

Some of God's best people knew, too: Moses, David, Solomon, John the Baptist, especially Jesus. We can follow in their footsteps as they lead us to the treasure of God's presence, revealed in the beauty of nature. Just as surely as He inhabits the people He created, the earth declares His majesty. Through it, God has delivered some of the clearest messages to date.

*Some of us are more predisposed to hearing God through nature than others. Would you call yourself a "nature girl"? If so, when did that love develop in you?

Read Psalm 65:5-6. What did David learn about God from mountains?

When you look at mountains, what does God communicate to you about Himself?

Since I was a little girl, my favorite retreat has always been the mountains. You may recall my first trip down a slope was a debacle, but my experiences steadily improved. We took our oldest son to Colorado for his first ski trip when he was four. Three years later, his second-grade teacher copied one of his writing assignments for me. Gavin wrote:

I went to Colarodo. On the way I saw some volcanos.

I was also on a bus. It seem'd like ther were ten millyon of them. I was a little scard becas maby one of them will explode! But none of them exploded. So I was safe.

Priceless! To a four-year-old, the volcanoes (formerly known as mountains) were staggering, even scary. Believer, when I stand high above the tree line with a fifty-mile view of the mountains formed by God, I know there is nothing He can't do. God communicates to me through the sheer magnitude of His power. If He can raise the mountains out of the ground with one word, He can lift my head when it's weary.

He tells me, "I think big." He's not a small God with small ideas. I spent a week last year in the mountains when a task before me seemed too large. I knew He'd tell me otherwise. It became clear as I stood twelve thousand feet high, a speck, not even discernable from the base, and surveyed the mountains. God said to me, "Yes, you are little, but you're standing on My mountain. Look what *I* can do."

He will be found in His mountains.

Read Psalm 65:7. What does God communicate to you through the oceans?

My Girlfriend Trina is an ocean girl, always has been, always will be. She would just as soon be around a dolphin as a human. Communicating to Trina, God once took her from the beach—crashing waves, squawking birds, strong winds—to underwater where she no longer had to masquerade as a person. Every sound was shut out. Every image was quieted. The beautiful fish swam slowly; a different pace emerged. And there was peace. In that moment, God said to her:

"I control entire worlds you can't even see. In My economy, peace always lurks just under what roars in your life. If you will lower yourself, be willing to let Me cover you, you will find the stillness that has eluded you."

He will be found in His oceans.

Read Psalm 65:8. What does God say to you through the sunrise and sunset? What do they proclaim to you?

Earlier, I mentioned the night my daughter began having seizures. We spent half the night in the ER while Sydney suffered through MRIs, blood tests, a spinal tap, CT scans, IVs. She was four, and it was horrific. On par with my dismay over her experience was my fear for her diagnosis. Was a gigantic tumor pressing on her brain? Was there some defect she'd never recover from? I wrote earlier about coming home that night, sobbing alone in my bed, unable to form a complete sentence of prayer.

Images of her botched spinal tap haunted me all night long. I heard her screams. I imagined the worst-case scenario at the neurologist's the next day. It was the longest night I've ever had.

I dragged myself out of bed early in the morning; sleep had proven elusive. I checked in on her, her daddy sleeping on the floor nearby, made sure she was breathing. I went downstairs and sat at my dining room table. The back of our house overlooks hill country so beautiful, I often marvel that God has allowed us to live here. As I looked into the darkness, numb and exhausted, the sun slowly began to rise. It broke through the top of the hills, and stunning colors filled the sky. I looked down at my arms, reflecting the pinks and oranges of sunrise, and felt the warmth on my face, and He spoke to me:

"Even the longest night is followed by a sunrise. If I can eliminate darkness, then I can handle your fears. I can handle Sydney's health. I can transform blackness into beauty: on this earth and in your life. And I will."

And He did.

He will be found in His sunrise and sunset.

⊙⊙ Read Psalm 65:9-11. Through the growth of the land, what does God communicate to you? About you? About Himself?

My dad grew up on a farm and took up the profession until he was thirty-one. He grew wheat and raised cattle in the plains of Kansas. As a city girl whose idea of a good crop refers to a new season of shoes at Nine West, I called Dad on this one.

He recounted a time in late summer one year when the cattle threatened to overgraze the range. He was short on hay, and winter was coming. The costly feed he normally reserved for winter was being used up, because the summer rains had run dry. Like all farmers, Dad began to wring his hands wondering how to make it all stretch.

About this time, Dad remembered how the clouds gathered and rolled across the sky, breaking open and showering his parched farm with rain. He nearly watched the alfalfa grow before his eyes. After the hay was mowed, baled, and stacked high in his barn, Dad stood there and breathed in the smell of fresh hay, rich and healthy. God spoke clearly as Dad surveyed the bounty of his land:

"I *will* take care of you. This was all Mine to begin with. I've only entrusted it to you. I'll help you tend it if you'll trust Me with the outcome. I am Lord of the Harvest."

A word we should take note of as mothers.

He will be found in the growth of His land.

David went on: grasslands, hills, meadows, flocks, valleys, grain. We could go on, too: forests, deserts, autumn, storms, wind, animals, planets, stars. Land sakes! The scope of creation declares God to be brilliant, beautiful, creative. The facets of His character are revealed in the diversity of His landscape.

*What is the clearest word you've ever received from God through creation?

When your ears get clogged, and His voice becomes fuzzy, Believer, go outside. Be in His world. It's like coming home. Even Jesus "went out to a mountainside to pray" (Luke 6:12). God's voice cannot be silenced in the breadth of creation. And know this: What God has revealed through the beauty of nature is just the tip of His iceberg. As our friend Job rightly declared of God's universe: "And these are but the outer fringe of his works; how faint the whisper we hear of him!" (Job 26:14).

If this is how God whispers, imagine what it will be like in the end, when "the Lord will roar from Zion and thunder from Jerusalem; the earth and the sky will tremble" (Joel 3:16). For now, those who will listen can hear His voice, but one day, it will not be denied.

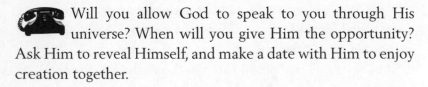 Will you allow God to speak to you through His universe? When will you give Him the opportunity? Ask Him to reveal Himself, and make a date with Him to enjoy creation together.

Silence

Our littlest, God bless him. We thought we'd birthed two extreme talkers until we had Caleb. His mouth opens the moment his eyes do, and it never shuts until sleep overtakes his desire to say "one more thing."

I remember one night as Caleb sat on Brandon's lap, talking incessantly while we were trying to have a conversation. "And Dad, tomorrow, I'm not going to school and me and you is going hunting. We'll be quiet and patient and get some deers. The mean kind with horns. And I will shoot a hippo. Then just me and you will eat it because it's ours and we're not going to share with Mommy. Can we, Dad? Can we hunt tomorrow? Can we stay for forty-five hours? Dad? Dad?"

The blood trickled out of Brandon's ears, and he snapped. I passed zero judgment, as I once told Brandon I'd welcome a nervous breakdown just to spend a few days in a quiet hospital. "CALEB! I want you to sit here for two minutes without saying *one single word!*" Caleb's eyes got big, and after five seconds his bottom lip started trembling. He burst out crying and proclaimed, "Buuut IIII haaavve tooo taaaalk tooo yooooooou!"

I'm positive God sometimes looks down from heaven and says, "Be quiet for two minutes and *just listen.*" As believers, we often talk and talk and talk, and wonder why we didn't hear anything from God. In His communication arsenal, God uses silence. It's not our favorite tool. We're not a silent people. We get uncomfortable and impatient. We're task-mastering Americans — every second counts. Yet God shows us a compelling history of productive silence in Scripture. Let's tune in by shutting up.

As we've studied, God used silence to communicate to Jesus, Zechariah, and Job. Constantly in Scripture, God silenced His people. Jesus silenced His enemies. Followers sat quietly and listened. Disciples fixed their ears and learned. Today, we'll look at how God turns silence into conversation.

Meditation. This often conjures up weird images of chanting and bare feet. Somehow meditation got mixed up with New Age ceremonies and yoga. In fact, meditation was first mentioned in Genesis and continues to be one of God's greatest tools today.

Read Psalm 119:27. What do you think this means? What do you make of the word "meditate"? It's all over the psalms.

In the Old Testament, there are two Hebrew words for meditation. *Haga* means to "utter, groan, meditate, or ponder." *Sihach* means to "muse, rehearse in one's mind, or contemplate." These words can also be translated as dwell, diligently consider, and heed.[1] Basically, meditation is deliberately thinking about God, Scripture, and your relationship to God and His words. Not twelve seconds of a passing thought, not an incidental consideration. But a set time to "be still, and know that I am God" (Psalm 46:10).

This time could easily be built into our daily Bible study.

In fact, that is the precise place for it. Problem is, we're doing good to squeeze in some reading and prayer. Thank you, but we don't have time for silence. Yet it is through our quietness the Spirit can teach us the depths of Scripture. He can dissect a passage for us and apply it to our hearts. Meditation is the gift of time; time we are not compelled to fill with our own ramblings and interpretations.

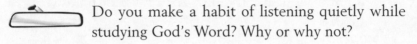 Do you make a habit of listening quietly while studying God's Word? Why or why not?

*Why is silence hard?

Meditation works like this for me: I secure a passage in my head, sometimes just one or two sentences, and I look up from my Bible. I allow the passage to roll around my brain. I let the Spirit start forming edges. Two things begin to connect, or one word starts to rise to the top, and I sense insight coming. I stay still and don't force it. I ask the Spirit to teach me, show me. I'm patient. I've been here many times before. My mind starts to close in on something. I start to see it. I stay focused. At once, I'm entirely engaged in the Scripture and entirely detached. I release what I "already know" or heard someone else say. I will not teach myself. I am a blank page. Show me, Spirit. The treasure starts to lift out. I want to rush it, but I might lose it. What are You teaching me? There. There it is. I see it. I get it. I didn't see it at first, but silence brought it into relief.

I hear God.

Without meditation, my understanding of God is relegated to what is already in my head. If I never give the Spirit time to show me new things, I can't grow in Him. We can no more expect to assimilate the Bible without meditation than we could become a doctor without listening in class.

There is an ancient art, once practiced by all Christians

though later associated with monks, called *lectio divina*, which literally means "sacred reading" but functionally means "listening for God." It offers a beautifully progressive format for embracing silence, communicating with God. It involves:

1. *Reading* a passage of Scripture slowly. Not gobbling down four chapters or speed-reading but slowly, attentively, gently listening for a word or phrase from God.
2. *Meditating* on that passage, repeating it maybe, allowing it to interact with your thoughts, hopes, memories, desires. Allowing God's corporate Word to become your personal Word.
3. *Praying* the Scripture and its fullness back to God, holding up your experiences to the light of God's Word, and offering obedience, submission, reverence.
4. *Contemplating*, in which you simply rest in God's presence as the One who has invited you there and used His Word to transform you; quiet rest after time well spent with God.

*Do you see any of these areas missing in your time with God? How might they strengthen your faith?

God's Word tells us that, without a healthy dose of silence before God, we may get forced into it. You know when you need to speak to your child, but she won't stop talking, and you clamp your hand over her mouth? Sometimes we leave God no other recourse.

📻 Read back over Luke 1:8-20. What would you guess
   Zechariah thought about in silence over the next nine
months?

How might his own talking have interfered?

In disciplining him, God gave Zechariah the opportunity
to do nothing but listen for nearly a year. He wasn't able to
talk with Mary for the three months she lived there. He didn't
get to tell Elizabeth what had happened in the temple. He
was alone with the knowledge of angels, prophecy, miracles,
ministry, redemption. I'd say he had plenty to meditate on.
God saw to it that he wouldn't become distracted. He doesn't
waste silence.

📻 Zechariah's first words demonstrate this. Read Luke
   1:67-79. How was all that silence productive?

God speaks through silence. When we become His quiet
audience willingly, He seizes the opportunity. Through discipline, He sometimes has to strike us speechless in order to
hear Him. It may sting at first, but He has something to say. It's
that hand clamping over our mouths, shocking us into silence.
As Elihu begged Job, "Listen! Listen to the roar of his voice, to
the rumbling that comes from his mouth" (Job 37:2).

*Has God ever rendered you speechless? How?
What did He say to you?

Stillness can combine with any of God's other communication tools: prayer followed by silence; Bible study enriched
by quietness; listening through conviction; sitting silently in
nature. Fundamentally, how can we expect to hear God at all
if we don't listen? When a space is created, God can open the
floodgates of heaven and shower us with conversation.

It's a beautiful place to sit quietly at God's feet and listen. It's where Jesus whispered His secrets to Mary while Martha banged pots in the kitchen. Martha Kilpatrick wrote in *Adoration*:

> Jesus stopped at Bethany one day and Martha bustled
> to fix his lunch and make him comfortable. She chose
> to relate to His humanity. . . . Martha would feed him.
> Mary stilled herself in homage before Him. She chose
> to relate to His divinity. . . .
>   Mary would feed *on* Him.[2]

"Be still, and know that I am God." (Psalm 46:10)

Do you need to be quiet, Believer? Has silence been a missing part of your communication with God? Commit to quietness before Him. Ask Him to clear your mind and speak His treasures. It will change your life.

Church

Sometimes in life you are unbiased. You are impartial. You're as neutral as Switzerland. It is within your ability to say, "Ask me. I'm an objective third party." I feel this way about soccer and the PTA. Though "unopinionated" is not an adjective that frequently gets wasted on me, it's occasionally true.

Today is not one of those days.

Today, we'll see how God is found in His church, and I'm about as impartial as the stage moms of four-year-old pageant girls. I spent my entire career as a fetus in church, and I never left it. My dad became a full-time minister when I was five. I grew up there three days a week, then promptly married a pastor. Church is a place where God drew me to Him and discipled me. It's where He booted me into ministry and showered me with godly friends. It has been the centerpoint of my life for as long as I can remember.

As in many of its other channels, God's voice has been muffled within His church, because, unfortunately, He had to commit it to mortals. Some gravitate to hellfire and brimstone while others are in the business of fluff. For these and myriad other reasons, church attendance steadily declined in the 1990s, and "new growth" consisted mainly of people moving from other churches. Disturbingly little church growth is attributable to new converts. Claims of prolific growth have been exaggerated, as the back door is as large as the front. Getting men engaged is harder than ever; women are almost twice as likely to be involved in a discipleship effort. When surveyed, the most pressing need pastors reported wasn't authentic worship or effective discipleship; it was addressing the apathy of their congregation.[3]

 Why do you think the church has fallen on such hard times?

Just as we've learned to find God in the image of mankind no matter how it has been distorted, we can find God in church regardless of its deficiencies. After all, it was called the "house of God" forty-nine times in Scripture. Talk about coming home.

One of my favorite churches referenced in the Bible was in Antioch. Now, Antioch was in Syria, about three hundred miles north of Jerusalem. It was on the northeast corner of the Mediterranean Sea and functioned as the great central point of Christianity as it spread after Jesus' resurrection. It was obviously a Gentile city, but Jesus eradicated the distinction of being Jewish. It was the capital of the Roman province in Asia and ranked third, after Rome and Alexandria, in importance.[4]

Read Acts 11:19-21. Why do you think most of these new Jewish converts only shared the gospel with other Jews they encountered? Why not with those who were different from them?

*In what ways does the modern church sometimes withhold the gospel from outsiders? Why do we end up looking like a holy huddle?

Thank goodness for "some of them" (verse 20). These few men had no problem sharing with the lost people of Antioch. Of course, they'd been driven there by persecution. You'd think they would've learned to shut their mouths; the gospel landed them in Syria in the first place. But you can't quench an unquenchable fire. The joy of salvation trumped the fear of persecution, and out of a godless Roman city rose a church to be reckoned with.

Somewhere, we've forgotten how Jesus said, "It is not the healthy who need a doctor, but the sick. I have not come to call the righteous, but sinners" (Mark 2:17). So many churches are little more than a holy huddle. It's all about saying the right things and putting on the God-face, and heaven forbid we have to deal with someone in sin. These days, you have to get your life together before you can walk in the doors of a church. Our first instinct is often judgment, if not straight to her face then behind her back. We disguise it as a "prayer request" to justify our gossip, but who is holding that believer's hand? Loving her toward restoration?

*Reread Acts 11:20-21. These Greeks didn't follow Jewish customs. They'd never observed all those Jewish laws. They had no history with God, yet His "hand was with them." What does this teach us about God's vision for the church?

If you're a skeptic, a new believer, or a saint, God's church is where He planned on speaking hope. Every word spoken there should encourage the weary and sustain the broken. The church is a hospital; Jesus made it clear. Through an obedient church, God speaks mercy. If all you hear is condemnation, Believer, those aren't God's words. Just as surely as shame helps us weed out the Enemy's voice, it identifies churches that are suffocating God's voice of mercy. A healthy church isn't a club of compromise, nor is it a den of judgment. You should be hearing God's kind voice loud and clear there.

🔊 Read Acts 11:22-24. Why do you think the Jerusalem church sent Barnabas to Antioch?

At the beginning of God's church, we see a beautiful instance of unity. The Jerusalem church was made up of all Jews; God's chosen people, the nation of Jesus. Their history with God went back two thousand years. And as the gospels declare, sharing their faith was a sticking point. It was their special treasure, and good luck prying it out of their fingers. Antioch bore the Roman stamp, sworn enemies of the Jews. As a whole, they aired their superior education and culture while rejecting the faith of Israel. While Antioch surely felt superior to little Jerusalem in little Judea, the Jews probably needed a gurney for the huge chip on their shoulder.

Yet they put aside their differences in favor of unity: They loved the same God. Jerusalem sent Barnabas, a rising star to encourage their new brothers in Christ. Antioch's gain was Jerusalem's loss; what a dear minister! They locked arms and chased after God's purposes, forsaking their own.

🔊 *God's hand of favor was clear. What is God communicating to you about unity among modern churches? Does He have a word for you?

Satan has done a number on the unity of the bride of Christ. Not only does He divide individuals in the local body, but he drives a wedge between churches. Something of a competition has developed. Who's better? Who's bigger? Whose worship sounds nicer? Which style is better? Which denomination is right? Whose pastor is superior? Whose building? Whose children's ministry? Whose parking lot? Whose bulletin?

Land o' livin'! The Enemy stirs the pot while we criticize

each other in ignorance. Believer, the term *body of Christ* does not just refer to individuals in the local church; it applies to the entire church. Your local church may be the arm, which works for all fingers and elbows and wrists that are drawn there. Mine may be the leg where the knees and toes can operate freely. "If they were all one part, where would the body be?" (1 Corinthians 12:19).

Thank goodness for our different styles and ministries and roles. We'd reach a lot less people if we were all the same. Some churches bring the gospel to the homeless in downtowns; others bring it to the wealthy driving Jaguars. It's all important because they all need Jesus. If one church deemed the ministry of another less worthy, there would be a smaller party in heaven one day.

Do you struggle with whole church unity? If so, how? What do you need to release?

Read Acts 11:25-26. At this point, why do you think Barnabas brought in Saul (soon known as Paul)?

Barnabas was the kind believer who convinced the disciples to welcome Saul. They were terrified of him, because before his conversion he had been a leader in the movement to lynch Jesus' followers. But Barnabas believed in him. He was Saul's first friend in the faith. Saul had been sent to Tarsus for protection, but Barnabas knew where to find him. It was good work to fetch this candle from under the bushel and set it in a candlestick. A slow burn turned into a raging inferno, and a preacher was born.

Oh, to be a member of *that* church! Can you imagine the wisdom God spoke through those two? He set this church ablaze through His ministers. Antioch became Paul's home; all three missionary journeys were launched from there. Not only was it home to the first Gentile church, but its members were first honored with the title we still bear proudly: *Christians.*

Believer, God's ministers are His mouthpiece. If you're in need of a word from Him, He'll meet you every Sunday morning in the sanctuary. God equips His pastors to speak on His behalf. There is hardly a clearer way to hear Him. Of course, you must saddle yourself to a church that preaches the gospel truth. Certainly any fool can plug in a microphone and call himself "Brother." That's why we're given discernment; the Spirit will tell you when to get the heck out of Dodge.

But to sit under the teaching of a godly leader, chosen by God, is to hear His voice. Plain and simple. For me, it has been the avenue of conviction, insight, and confirmation more times than I can number.

*What is a clear word you've received from God through the mouth of a minister? If your answer is "none," why do you think that is?

I realize every church has its problems. You know, church would be perfect if it wasn't for all the people. But people we are, so we have to choose compassion over criticism. Believer, rather than focus on the deficiencies of church, let's remember that it's God's platform from which to speak. To you. To me. He has the ability to strip away all the parts we get wrong, and still pierce your heart with truth every Sunday. That's not to mention the other six days the church becomes His megaphone. In the pursuit of God's voice, embrace the church, warts and all.

That's just the way God loves us.

Do you need to clear the air with God about His church? Do you need to get in one? Ask for guidance in this area. Commit to listening closely for God's voice through your church. Covet what He has to say.

People

Right after college, Brandon accepted his first staff position at Southern Hills Baptist Church in Tulsa. In addition to my first year of teaching, I landed myself a second job: pastor's wife. What did I know? I was twenty-two. That was back when I thought I had to volunteer in every ministry and attend every activity. After all, I was a pastor's wife—we do everything well, and we love it all, and we never feel cranky.

That first year, a little conference came to town that our women's ministry was going to. You might have heard of it: Women of Faith. Just a small affair. I did *not* want to go. I saw the flyer. It was a bunch of old women. Two days of listening to grandmas. But I was a happy new pastor's wife, so off I went. Of course, I laughed so hard a couple of times, I think I wet myself a little. The old women talked about boobs. I couldn't believe my good luck.

One of the speakers told of her son overseas, serving in the military. He was young, across the world, lonely. Aching to love on him, she called in a favor from a friend who was visiting his area. She said, and I'll never forget this: "I just needed someone with skin on to love him."

Girls, with all the affection of the universe God has for us, I believe He gave us each other because sometimes we need someone with skin on. We need an arm around our neck. We need someone to hold our hand. Our ears need to hear someone say, "I'll help you." God's love is reflected in the counsel of His people.

From the beginning of humanity, people served as God's mouthpiece. He sent Elihu to Job, Moses to Pharoah, Nathan to David, Nehemiah to Artaxerxes, Jeremiah to Judah, Ananias to Saul, Peter and Paul to the Jerusalem Council. I've saved this one for last, because it is the most common way God speaks in the Word: through people.

God ordains counsel from two sources:

Plans fail for lack of counsel,
     but with many advisers they succeed. (Proverbs 15:22)

"The Counselor, the Holy Spirit, whom the Father will send in my name, will teach you all things." (John 14:26)

How must these two intersect?

We sometimes mistakenly say, "Well, that's her counsel, but what does God think?" Now counselors must be chosen well—after all, "Blessed is the man who does not walk in the counsel of the wicked" (Psalm 1:1). But God's history shows us that He sends His very words through people. That *is* God speaking. Hearing the Spirit takes practice, maturity. God knows it. In the spirit of clarity, He frequently sends someone with skin on. It's easier to hear. Harder to confuse.

*Has God ever spoken to you through another believer? What did He say?

I've been counseled my entire life. When God has a message for me, I cannot escape it. It's what I read in the Word, it's what the Spirit presses on me, it seems the only thing anyone wants to say to me. Often when I've been privately dealing with an issue, God sends a person to nail the coffin shut. They'll bring it up or have a strong word about it, and I throw my hands up and say, "OKAY, GOD!"

I've been on the other end, too. Sometimes my counsel is sought out, and it's weird how the words are given to me. I find myself saying things I don't know experientially, but I'm sure of them. Other times, I'm practically forced to seek someone out, give him or her a word. This is often met by tears or shock. "How did you know?" I didn't. It's how God speaks.

 *Read 2 Corinthians 5:16-18. What do you think our ministry of reconciliation involves?

How would a worldly point of view taint this ministry?

Matthew Henry wrote, "By the mediation of Jesus Christ, [God] has reconciled the world to himself, and put himself into a capacity of being actually reconciled to offenders, without any wrong or injury to his justice or holiness, and does not impute to men their trespasses."[5] The breach was restored, better than it was before. Because of Jesus, we stand in clean fellowship with God. The Holy Spirit resides within us. The freedom we live in goes beyond description. "All this is from God," and in light of our privileges, each of us has been appointed a minister.

Read 2 Corinthians 5:19-20. We're flawed. We struggle. Why do you think God made us His spokespeople?

Do you know what we have the privilege of doing through our ministry? We help reconcile broken hearts with wholeness. We get to help restore a damaged faith. We help piece back together a fractured relationship. We point people toward good paths and warn them of dangerous ones. We help repair the shattered identity of a friend. We know a Guy.

Believer, we get to walk the lost into the arms of their Savior. What could be more worthy? God committed this ministry to you and me as though "he was making his appeal through us." We are God's fellow workers (2 Corinthians 6:1). We're not Plan B when He can't get His word across any other way. He has faith in us. After all, He did make us in His image. If we can bear His character, then we can deliver His word.

Paul goes on to qualify the effectiveness of this ministry. To be sure, the right counsel brings victory, but the wrong counsel brings destruction. Believers are daily persuaded toward ruin in "God's name." History brims with accounts of charismatic leaders gathering the gullible, citing divine visions. Though they contradict God's Word, cult leaders lead astray millions. On a lesser scale, a believer out of fellowship, out of the Word, and out of line still has the ability to open her mouth and say, "If you want my advice. . . ."

Read 2 Corinthians 6:3-10. How does God want us to conduct "our ministry"?

Paul gave three fantastic reasons for living as such:

1. To put no stumbling block in anyone's path—that is, in the path of anyone who seeks your counsel or looks to your life as an example.
2. So your ministry won't be discredited; it won't be fodder for ridicule or a platform for hypocrisy.
3. Because you are a servant of God, nothing less than His ambassador.

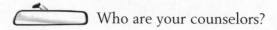 Who are your counselors?

Have they counseled you well? What makes you say that?

*What qualities in this passage do they exhibit best?

If you don't have at least one counselor like this, what can you do about that?

As believers, sometimes we're the counselor; other times we seek it out. It is a wise woman who brings her decisions and struggles to a godly friend. Because the Holy Spirit lives within us, He can open our mouths and speak directly. When godly counsel lines up with God's Word and the Spirit delivers peace, you know you're heading in the right direction. It is an honor that God uses us so vitally. Though we misunderstand it, God's people are His treasure, His delight, even His mouthpiece. We must faithfully deliver God's Word and gratefully receive it through our brothers and sisters in Christ.

We proclaim him, admonishing and teaching everyone with all wisdom, so that we may present everyone perfect in Christ. To this end I labor, struggling

with all his energy, which so powerfully works in me.
(Colossians 1:28-29)

Do you need to evaluate your counselors? Are they equipped as God's mouthpiece? Ask the Spirit to show you truth. Commit to your own ministry of reconciliation. Pray for the opportunities to speak on God's behalf.

Tune In

Girls, I pray you've discovered that God's voice is not a mystery. He no more wants to trick you than you do your own children. His voice communicates constantly—sometimes about you, other times about Him. As obedient children, we're interested in all of it. There is nothing God won't do to talk to you.

I'm a big fan of recapping. I've experienced profound insight in God's Word and been unable to recall it the next day. Entire years of my life have also been sacrificed to a faulty memory. Thank goodness for cameras, or my kids' baby faces would surely fall into obscurity. I know reviewing takes a little time, but it proves invaluable for getting truth to stick. So for the following points, go back through your book and list the biggest takeaway for each:

- Seeking God's whole will
- When God is silent
- Discerning between God's voice and other voices

God's voice through:

- His Word
- Prayer
- Fasting
- Worship
- Mankind, made in
  His image
- Friendship
- Marriage
- Parenthood
- Spiritual gifts
- Dreams and visions

- Conviction and
  obedience
- Humility
- Spiritual warfare
- Suffering
- Discipline
- Peace
- Creation
- Silence
- Church
- People

Look over that list, Believer. Wasn't that worth your time? It was definitely worth God's. I hope you understand how many opportunities He has given you to hear Him. In humility, we'll never want for God's voice. While some of these modes of communication are initiated by Him, there are plenty in that list you can immerse yourself in any old day. God has made it nearly impossible *not* to hear Him.

This side of heaven, there is nothing sweeter than communion with the Creator. Although it seems stunning that He'd draw so close to us, history tells us it's true. May your experiences confirm indeed that "God's voice thunders in marvelous ways; he does great things beyond our understanding" (Job 37:5).

Be the listener He seeks.

Thank God for this journey. Praise Him for what He has revealed to you along the way. Ask for the lines of communication between you to be forever open until you see each other face to face.

Leader's Guide

For this study, each woman will need:

1. A copy of *Tune In*
2. A Bible (all references included come from the *New International Version*, but another version is fine)
3. A journal or notebook with lined paper

Tune In is a six-week study. Each week requires five days of work. Women will spend approximately thirty minutes on each day of Bible study.

Each week delves deeply into the Bible, what it meant when it was written as well as what it means now. All historical context is provided, but it's always helpful if the leader has some familiarity with the passages. I suggest having leaders stay at least a week ahead in the study in order to offer advance guidance if necessary. The ideal size for a small group is eight to twelve women.

In my church, the whole women's ministry gathers as a large group each week (for worship and a brief teaching session), then women divide into small groups to discuss the study. In other words, all the small groups meet in the same building at the same time. In this case, I've found it helpful to have a leaders' meeting each week just before the large session. Fifteen minutes together in prayer and discussion have addressed many issues before they came up in small groups. Leaders can discuss complicated questions and anticipate weekly challenges in advance.

If the small groups meet in separate places, like homes, perhaps you can have a weekly online dialogue, or pair up leaders so they have a partner to encourage. Supported leaders are happier leaders.

The small group discussion should take sixty to ninety minutes, depending on the size and personality of the small group. Feel free to supplement that time with worship, activities, or a large group session.

Each week, set the example by having your Bible and book open and ready. Begin each session with prayer, asking God to inhabit your conversation and increase your faith.

Have your girls open their books to Days 1–4. The questions marked with an asterisk (*) are good discussion questions to pose. There are two to four of them marked in each day of study. Look ahead at the designated questions to prepare adequately for discussion. Most of the questions selected involve the personal application of the study, but by all means keep bringing in the Scripture and history that set it up. Each week features a powerful story with fascinating details. Be sure to include them within discussion. But if your group obviously wants to pursue a different point, don't squash the Spirit's leading. Create an atmosphere of authenticity by voicing your own thoughts and struggles. Keep conversation moving, and work hard to include all four days in discussion. If you aim to spend roughly fifteen minutes on each day's questions, Days 1–4 will take about an hour to cover.

When Days 1–4 have been discussed, refer to Day 5. As this is a personal prayer and journal activity, wrap up your conversation by asking, "What was the biggest thing you took away from this day? This week? What did the Spirit teach you in prayer and journaling?"

Close each weekly session in prayer. This would be a great time to change your prayer techniques each week.

- Try partner praying one week—two girls share immediate needs and pray over each other.
- You could lead the group in sentence prayer—only *one* or *two* sentences voiced at a time ("Thank You for speaking to me through worship." "Help me to hear Your voice in suffering."). Explain this technique first, and model it by beginning with one prayer sentence. When you think the girls are done, close in a brief final prayer.
- You could lead them through silent prayer using prompts from Scripture. For example, open to Psalm 66. Read verses 1-4 aloud and say, "Praise God for His awesome deeds in your life. Who has He been for you?" Give group members two or three minutes to pray silently, then read verses 5-7 and say, "How has God delivered you? What has He done on your behalf?" Allow them to pray silently and continue through Scripture prompts as you see fit. This can be done with any passage you are drawn to or one that seems to uniquely fit your group.
- You could pray Scripture. Choose a passage like Psalm 33 or Exodus 15:1-18. Have each woman open her Bible to the chosen passage. Tell the group that you will read the whole passage aloud, then they will choose a line or phrase they'd like to pray again to God ("In your unfailing love, You will lead the people You have redeemed"). Allow them to speak various verses randomly as God leads them. They might speak several times each over the course of the prayer. When it seems they are done, close briefly with a final prayer.
- If your group is small enough, you could try intercessory prayer. Take turns praying over each group member individually. For example, put Jen in the middle. Each woman in turn prays two or three sentences over her.

Think "brief." Then move to Sarah and pray over her individually. It is a special way for your small group to connect with God in sweet intercession.

- Brainstorm with the other leaders on various prayer techniques. This is a wonderful place to teach creative prayer by example. Anything goes as long as God's name is honored.

Consider a celebration, dinner, party, day trip, or anything fun at the close of the study. *Tune In* is a journey taken together. Your girls will have shared, cried, learned from each other. God called us His family. You know He loves to see the kids getting along. Small groups should foster fellowship as much as learning.

I love group cohesion, and I'm a big fan of longevity with the same girls. My own personal small group has been together three years, and it just keeps getting better. Where we are now together compared to where we began cannot even be compared. We began as students of the Word (mostly strangers), and now we're sisters.

Karla Worley put it like this in *Traveling Together*:

How can you, my friend in the faith, help me to become more like Christ? You can know me. You can be there. Hold me accountable for holy living. Encourage me to live the life of the Spirit. Model servanthood. Keep me active in worship and service. And you can do all this in the course of our days and years together, not just doing holy things, but understanding that all the things we do hold the possibility of the holy.[1]

Leaders, nurture friendships. Create authenticity. Make opportunities for real connection available. The longer you laugh and cry and pray together, the stronger this journey gets.

Notes

WEEK ONE: SAY WHAT?

1. Dallas Willard, *Hearing God: Developing a Conversational Relationship with God* (Downers Grove, IL: InterVarsity, 1999), 18.
2. Billy Graham, *Just As I Am* (San Francisco: HarperSanFrancisco, 1997), 63.
3. Henry and Richard Blackaby, *Hearing God's Voice* (Nashville: Broadman, Holman, 2002), 46.
4. Willard, 33.
5. E. Stanley Jones, *A Song of Ascents* (Nashville: Abingdon, 1979), 190.
6. Willard, 178.
7. George Muller, *The Autobiography of George Muller* (Springdale, PA: Whitaker House, 1984), 139–140.

WEEK TWO: HE SPEAKS THROUGH DISCIPLINES

1. Josephus, *Antiquities*, 18.5.2; see also "Machaerus," *Bible History Online*, http://www.bible-history.com/geography/ancient-israel/machaerus.html.
2. Matthew Henry, "Commentary on Luke 7," *Matthew Henry Complete Commentary on the Whole Bible*, http://bible.crosswalk .com/Commentaries/MatthewHenryComplete/mhc-com .cgi?book=lu&chapter=007.
3. James Orr, MA, DD, general editor, "The Lord's Prayer," *The International Standard Bible Encyclopedia*, http://www .searchgodsword.org/enc/isb/view.cgi?number=T5576.
4. Frederick B. Meyer, *The Secret of Guidance* (Chicago: Moody, 1997), 43.

5. Dallas Willard, *Hearing God: Developing a Conversational Relationship with God* (Downers Grove, IL: InterVarsity, 1999), 203.

6. Bill Bright, "Your Personal Guide to Fasting and Prayer," *Campus Crusade Ministries*, 1997, http://www.billbright.com/howtofast/.

7. "The Sanctuary," *Bible History Online*, http://www.bible-history .com/gentile_court/TEMPLECOURTpop_The_Sanctuary.htm.

Week Three: He Speaks Through People

1. Matthew Henry, "Commentary on Genesis 1," *Matthew Henry Complete Commentary on the Whole Bible*, http://bible.crosswalk .com/Commentaries/MatthewHenryComplete/mhc-com .cgi?book=ge&chapter=001.

2. Dallas Willard, *Hearing God: Developing a Conversational Relationship with God* (Downers Grove, IL: InterVarsity, 1999), 32–33.

3. Karla Worley, *Traveling Together* (Birmingham, AL: New Hope Publishers, 2003), 19, 29.

4. "Betrothed," *Bible History Online*, http://www.bible-history.com/ jesus/jesusuntitled00000273.htm.

5. William Makepeace Thackeray, *Quoteland.com*, http://www .quoteland.com/topic.asp?CATEGORY_ID=209.

6. Matthew Henry, "Commentary on Luke 2," *Matthew Henry Complete Commentary on the Whole Bible*, http://bible.crosswalk .com/Commentaries/MatthewHenryComplete/mhc-com .cgi?book=lu&chapter=002.

Week Four: He Speaks Through His Spirit

1. Henry and Richard Blackaby, *Hearing God's Voice* (Nashville: Broadman, Holman, 2002), 24.

2. Matthew Henry, "Commentary on Daniel 9," *Matthew Henry Complete Commentary on the Whole Bible*, http://bible.crosswalk .com/Commentaries/MatthewHenryComplete/mhc-com .cgi?book=da&chapter=009.

3. "The Benefits of the Babylonian Captivity," *Bible History Online*, http://www.bible-history.com/map_babylonian_captivity/map_of

_the_deportation_of_judah_the_benefits_of_the_babylonian
_captivity.html.

WEEK FIVE: HE SPEAKS THROUGH CIRCUMSTANCES

1. Lawrence O. Richards, *Illustrated Bible Handbook* (Nashville: Nelson, 1997), 244; NIV Study Bible (Grand Rapids, MI: Zondervan, 2002), 722.
2. *NIV Study Bible*, 723.
3. Matthew Henry, "Commentary on Job 33," *Matthew Henry Complete Commentary on the Whole Bible*, http://bible.crosswalk .com/Commentaries/MatthewHenryComplete/mhc-com .cgi?book=job&chapter=33.

WEEK SIX: GOD HAUNTS

1. "Christian Meditation: Is it Really Christian?" *All About God*, http:// www.allaboutgod.com/christian-meditation.htm.
2. Martha Kilpatrick, *Adoration* (Jacksonville, FL: SeedSowers Publishing, 1999), 17.
3. George Barna, *Boiling Point* (Ventura, CA: Regal, 2001), 236–237, 242.
4. "Antioch," *Bible History Online*, http://www.bible-history.com/ eastons/A/Antioch/.
5. Matthew Henry, "Commentary on 2 Corinthians 5," *Matthew Henry Complete Commentary on the Whole Bible*, http://bible.crosswalk .com/Commentaries/MatthewHenryComplete/mhc-com.cgi?book= 2co&chapter=005.

LEADER'S GUIDE

1. Karla Worley, *Traveling Together* (Birmingham, AL: New Hope Publishers, 2003), 43.

About the Author

Jen has partnered with her husband, Brandon, in full-time ministry for eleven years while keeping her vow to never wear suntan pantyhose and white flats. If you catch her in either of those, please contact her Girlfriends immediately so they can stage an intervention. Although she has purchased either a new outfit or new shoes every single time she's been invited as a speaker, she is still happily married after twelve years (to the same man). Although Jen lives in beautiful Austin, Texas, she has somehow avoided becoming a runner, a bicyclist, a granola, or an earth-conscious recycler.

Jen intensely loves God, Jesus, her church, Scripture, writing, teaching, women, and finding the funny and profound in all these things. She surrounds herself with friends who, if not technically insane, are at least reassuringly dysfunctional. If nothing else, their lives provide amusing anecdotes should her own family ever become normal. However, her three kids—Gavin, Sydney Beth, and Caleb—have definitively squashed any notion that her life will ever be normal (see all stories included in this study). She recently crossed the threshold into her thirties, feigning indifference, where she now happily resides as a pretend grown-up.

Her first book, *A Modern Girl's Guide to Bible Study*, is also published by NavPress. Also available is her Bible study *Road Trip: Five Adventures You're Meant to Live*. Jen has two more Bible studies in the works.

For more information on Jen's ministry or to schedule her for your conference, retreat, or speaking engagement, go to www.jenhatmaker.com. You can also write to her at 7509 Callbram Lane, Austin, Texas 78736.

The common cure for a dull Bible study.

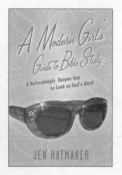

A Modern Girl's Guide to Bible Study
Jen Hatmaker   978-1-57683-891-4

Like a refreshing conversation between friends, *A Modern Girl's Guide to Bible Study* is fun and entertaining. It takes the academic nature of Bible study and blends it with humorous stories and thoughtful insights to help you uncover the life-changing truths of God's Word.

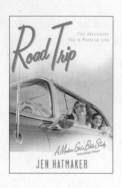

Road Trip
Jen Hatmaker   978-1-57683-892-1

Road trips are as much about the journey as they are their ultimate destinations, and who better to travel with than your best Girlfriends? You navigate life together, why not the Bible? Guided by Abraham, the Samaritan woman, Peter, Paul, and Jesus Himself, you're guaranteed the trip of a lifetime!

To order copies, call NavPress at 1-800-366-7788
or log on to www.navpress.com.

Discipleship Inside Out™